Property With Purpose

MICHAEL SHAW is a property investor, entrepreneur, and award-winning financial services professional. As an Investment Buyers Agent, Michael brings over two decades of experience and Masters' level qualifications across business, finance & financial planning, mortgage broking, and real estate.

After buying his first property in 2006, at the age of 18 — without any financial assistance, using the proceeds from an underground rave — Michael went on to build a $4mil portfolio while travelling to over 70 countries. Now, he's on a mission to empower 100,000 everyday Australians, whether new or savvy investors, to build wealth and create a life that serves them and their family.

Michael resides in his dream family home on beachside acreage near Bribie Island, QLD, with his beautiful wife Sarah, their boys Maximus and Lucas, their British Bulldog, Bruce, and their Rottweiler, Rosie.

If you don't find Michael on the golf course, in an Mixed Martial Arts gym, or on a 4WD camping adventure with his family, then you can find him at *www.avidhawks.com.au*

Property With Purpose

From 9-5 to Financial Freedom,
One Step at a Time.

MICHAEL SHAW

Published in Australia by Genreless Books
Sharing stories by independent Australian writers, of all genres.
genreless.com.au

First hardcover edition February 2026
ISBN 978-1-7643138-2-7

Lovingly designed and typeset by Liam Stritt
Set in Adobe Clean Serif 11/19.5pt
liamstritt.com

Contents

Foreword

Why This Book, Why Now

We've never lived in a more opportunity-rich time, but most people are still sitting on the sidelines twiddling their thumbs and being manipulated into thinking they're a victim to a situation that has been created in their own head.

People would rather complain, protest, and point their fingers at an imaginary enemy, rather than sitting down for a moment and listening to the *enemies* story, learning their skills and doing the work they did to achieve everything they have ever wanted.

If this life is so hard today, then why are so many millennials and Gen Z saying it's the *easiest* time in history?

Every day, Australians are manipulated into thinking that owning property is out of reach. The media runs *'click-bait'* style headlines about housing unaffordability, interest rates, and economic uncertainty. Dinner conversations circle around how *"the dream is dead,"* and social media is full of outrage and despair. We're all massively divided. But the truth is, in every so-called crisis, there's always some people who crush it and others who are left behind. While some wait and wish, others act and own.

Right now, Millennials and Gen Z have the tools, access, and leverage to create real generational wealth, if they choose to. Way more than their parents could have ever achieved. We live in an era where 26-year-old Melanie Perkins built Canva into a $10 billion business from a laptop in Perth. Where Morgan Hipworth built a donut company in Melbourne worth $200 million by the time he was 20 years old. And where investors like Eddie Dilleen, who bought his first property as a teenager working at McDonald's, now control portfolios worth tens of millions, all through residential real estate.

These aren't flukes. They're examples of what's possible when mindset meets strategy, and when people stop waiting for permission.

I wrote this book because I've lived both sides of the story.

I know what it's like to work a full-time job, to trade time for money, to feel like you're getting ahead very slowly, if at all. I didn't have a silver spoon (in fact in 2017, I desperately tried to convince my parents to be the guarantor for a loan and they refused). But you know what I did have? I had a drive to learn, to act, and to take calculated risks. My journey into property wasn't perfect or glamorous, but it was real. And over time, one property became two, then three, and eventually a portfolio that changed my future.

As I write this book, I'm 37 years old, we're now living in our acreage *forever* family home with my beautiful wife and soulmate, Sarah & our two little boys, Max & Lucas.

This book is for the everyday person who wants to break free from the ordinary.

It's not for people looking for a shortcut. It's not about instant wealth. It's about building real, tangible assets that generate income and grow in value, so you can eventually buy back your time, live on your terms, and leave something behind that actually matters.

This moment in time is a gift, but only if you act on it.

Millennials and Gen Z are the most empowered generations in history: We can learn more from YouTube in a weekend than previous generations learned in a year, we can buy property interstate, off-market, or under value from our phones...I've done it. And, we can access buyer's agents, brokers, and strategists who used to be reserved for the ultra-wealthy.

And yet, too many people are still waiting; waiting for the market to drop, waiting for the perfect property, waiting to feel "ready." Or even worse, waiting to save their way to their dream home that continues to move further and further out of reach every year.

Here's the truth, you can still buy the dream home in the same suburb or city your parents raised you in. But if you want to achieve those dreams in 2025, you need to stop taking 1950's advice.

The people building mega property portfolios aren't necessarily the smartest people. They're just the ones who started, stayed disciplined and understood that **property is a marathon, not a sprint.**

What This Book Will Give You

This book isn't about theory, it's a real-world guide based on *lived experience* (sorry, I hate that term) and proven principles. Whether you're starting from scratch or trying to scale, it will show you everything you need to know from an abundance mindset, how to buy your first property, mistakes to avoid, how to structure your portfolio so you don't make any unnecessary donations to the tax man, how to think like a business owner and build long term wealth on your terms.

Most importantly, it's going to show you that the life you want, the one where you no longer depend on a paycheck, the one where your assets work harder than you do, is not only possible, it's already being done by people just like you.

It's time to think bigger.

The real risk isn't in buying a property, it's in doing nothing.

If you're ready to take control of your financial future, to stop waiting and start building, then this book was written for you.

Let's get started.

Introduction

My Story:
From 9-5 to a $4mil Property Portfolio

Still to this day, I haven't heard a crazier story about someone buying their first property.

I was 17 years old (nearly 18), fresh out of school, obsessed with DJing Hardstyle, Hardcore, and any other genre you'd hear at a rave. I was on my way to Schoolies in Byron Bay. Life back then was beautifully simple.

Just before I left, my eldest brother asked, "What are you going to do now that school's finished?" He worked in insurance at the time, and knowing I was 100% done with traditional education and had no interest in University, I can now see he was probably asking out of concern. I replied, "I have no idea. I'm going to Schoolies, and I'll think about it when I get back."

Schoolies was chaos, a week of underage teenagers cutting loose. We basically hired out an entire caravan park and partied for days. It was probably the last time I truly had no responsibilities, no plan, and not a care in the world beyond drinking beers with my best mates and trying (mostly unsuccessfully) to talk to girls.

When I flew back to Sydney, I got a call from a woman I didn't recognise.

"Hi, is this Michael?" she asked.

"Yes..."

"Hi Michael, it's [Name] calling from [Company]." I forgot both as soon as she said them. "You recently applied for the job we advertised, and we were wondering if you'd like to come in for an interview."

My first thought was: *Did I?*

Second thought: *How hard did I party this week that I've completely forgotten applying for a job?*

Third thought: *I don't even know how to apply for a job...*

But what came out of my mouth was, "Yes, that would be great."

We locked in Thursday, 8:30am, Sydney CBD.

So Thursday rolls around and I'm sitting in the reception of this building, trying to work out who they are or even what industry they're in. There were no signs. The walls were exposed with visible scaffolding instead of proper plaster, and the door to the office was covered in plastic and tape. It felt more like a construction site than a company. But I needed a job, so I went with it.

The first question they asked was, "So Michael, why do you think you'd be good for this job?"

Keep in mind, I still had absolutely no idea what the job even was.

"Well," I said, "I've always worked well in a team, but I can also be shown something once and never forget it. I'm easy to get along with, I'm punctual, and I'll become a valuable member of your team."

It was all I could come up with on the spot, but it sounded a lot better than the truth: *"I've got no idea what this job is, I was probably drunk when I applied, and I've just come back from a week at Schoolies, so I'm broke."*

The whole interview went for about 15 minutes. Both ladies smiled and seemed enthusiastic about me starting. I got the job. Starting Monday. 8:30am. Salary? $25,000 a year.

Originally, I wanted to be a chef. I'd done hospitality in Years 11 and 12, and I enjoyed cooking. Still do. But during my work placement, I asked someone how much I'd earn starting out. The answer? Around $13,000 a year, working Friday and Saturday nights and Sunday afternoons.

Then these people offer me $25,000 to sit at a desk, Monday to Friday, 9 to 5. I mean, come on, no-brainer, right? Every time I see those reels on Instagram that ask, *"How much money did someone offer you to give up on your dream?"* my answer is always: **$25,000.**

That Friday night, I'm out with my brother and his mates. I tell them, "Oh yeah, I got a job."

"You got a job?!"

"Yeah."

"That's awesome, doing what?"

"I have no idea."

They burst out laughing.

"What do you mean you don't know?"

"I mean, I have no idea what the job is. I tried to find the company name at the interview or at least what the job was, but couldn't see anything."

Their laughter got louder.

"Well, what industry is it?"

"I genuinely don't know. All I know is that if I turn up Monday at 8:30am, they'll pay me $25,000 a year."

It reminded me of that *Seinfeld* episode "The Revenge" where George Costanza just starts turning up at his old job pretending he still works there. The only difference is, I had a real job. I just had no idea what it was.

A few beers later, one of the boys says he's starting a job soon and describes where it is. I'm like, "Hang on... I think we're in the same building." Then it all clicks.

Turns out, my brother's friend was starting at a new Workers' Compensation insurer setting up shop in Sydney. That weird office I'd been to was their temporary HQ while their North Sydney office was being renovated. While I was off partying at Schoolies, my brother had written me a resume (Thanks bro! I had zero academic achievements, just a part-time job and a few footy trophies), and applied for a bunch of jobs on my behalf.

Forever grateful. As much as I ended up hating insurance, it gave me the start I needed.

So Monday rolls around. I show up at 8:30am, and it turns out I'm the mailroom boy.

Back then, everyone still used mail and faxes, and it was my job to sort them and deliver them to everyone's desks. Because the company hadn't officially launched yet, the only people working there were the CEO, the GM, a few team leaders, the receptionist, and me. Not bad for an 18-year-old. I was literally rubbing shoulders with the top dogs. Imagine being invited to lunch by the CEO at 18. It doesn't happen.

A week later, they started hiring "Case Managers" and then "Assistant Case Managers" for their Claims department. Not exactly a huge promotion, but definitely a step up from the mailroom.

I asked my boss if I could apply.

"You've only been here a week!" she said.

"Does that mean I can't apply?"

"Well... no, I guess not."

So I applied. And who interviews me? My brother's best mate.

I had an earring and an eyebrow ring at the time, and he looked me dead in the eye and asked, "You gonna get rid of that sh*t if we hire you?"

"Uh... yeah, for sure. I can do that."

After a bit of banter, he bursts out laughing.

"Mate, you had the job before you walked in. You're hired."

I went back to my boss and told her *I'd be starting my new job in two weeks*. Back to the drawing board for her.

This really kicked off my 9-5 career in insurance.

I always look back at those times when I was 18 with a smile on my face. My brother and his mates helped me a lot getting started. Not just career wise but also helped me at 11:30pm on Fridays when I had literally run out of money so they paid for my beers for the rest of the night and paid for my train ticket home. Good times!

Now, my time in insurance did eventually come to an end (which we'll get to later), but I've got to admit, that job did something that changed my life. It put me on the path to becoming a property investor.

One night, I was getting ready to DJ at a club when Mum cornered me for another one of those "life talks."

"Now that you're working, you really need to think about buying a property," she said.

"Yeah, yeah..." I shrugged, clearly not interested.

"Well, you need to live somewhere. You can't live with Mum and Dad forever."

I fired back: "You had me, maybe you should've thought about that before having a third kid."

That pretty much sums up exactly where I was at in life. I wasn't ready for 'adult' conversations. Not even close.

Realistically, I wasn't ready for real 'adult' conversations until my late 20s. I just made the first of the 3-4 good decisions I needed to make at 18, I bought a property and held onto it.

But these conversations didn't stop. They dragged on for months. At this point, both of my older brothers had moved out, one at 24, the other at 20, and I was 18, nearly 19, still living at home and getting serious pressure to follow suit.

Looking back, I reckon they wanted to sell the big family home, but were just waiting for me to move out. Actually, now that I think about it... that's exactly what happened. I bought my first property, and they had a "For Sale" sign out the front within a year.

One night, after months of brushing it off, I finally caved and sat down with Mum.

"Alright. This property thing. How do we do it?"

I told them I wanted to live around Ryde, most of my mates were from there, so it seemed perfect. We started looking at apartments, and prices were hovering between $280,000 and $350,000. But on my current salary of $25,000 a year, with interest rates sitting around 8–9%, there was just no way.

We worked out I'd need to earn around $45,000 income and have about $25,000 saved for a deposit before I'd even stand a chance. Taking into consideration Government incentives that were offered at the time.

Then Mum hit me with the line that nearly ended the whole conversation:

"You'll need to stop going out so you can save for at least a couple of years."

Warning lights. Sirens. Abort mission.

"Yeah, nah. That's not happening," I said. "I'm sorry, Mum, but if I have to stop going out just to buy a house, then I'm not buying a house. End of story."

And I walked away. My parents must have thought I was destined to live at home forever.

But even though I bailed on that convo, something shifted. Over the next few weeks, the thought of buying a property kept bouncing around my head. I knew it was something I wanted, a goal I genuinely cared about, but I wasn't willing to give up the best part of my life at that time, going out with my mates.

Then one night I had my lightbulb moment.

It was a Friday. I was DJing at Sublime (Subbies) at Home Nightclub in Sydney. That venue was packed. Entry was $25, and there were easily 1,000–1,500 people inside.

I remember standing behind the decks, looking around and thinking:

25 bucks a head... 1,000 people... that's $25,000 in one night.

Then it hit me: *I'll just put on an event. Simple!*

After my set, I walked straight up to the promoter who'd booked me.

"Dude, how did you do this?" I asked, gesturing to the crowd.

"Do what?" he said.

"Like, this event. Like, how do you even make something like this happen?"

"You mean... promote and run your own party?"

"Yeah," I said, trying to sound cooler than I felt. "I'm actually thinking about doing one."

"Alright," he said. "Come over to mine and I'll run you through everything: costs, logistics, how to make it work."

"Done."

And just like that, my world cracked wide open. This crazy idea just landed in my lap. I'd never been more focused on a goal in my life.

I felt like Wayne in *Wayne's World 2* when Jim Morrison comes to him in a dream and tells him to put on a rock concert. He wakes up, clueless about where to start, but determined. Morrison even tells him the name of the guy who can help make it happen. For me, that promoter was my "Del Preston." I was going to put on a concert.

I know it sounds ridiculous, but that was genuinely how I saw it at the time. My inspiration came from movies like *Wayne's World*, *Dumb and Dumber*, and *Forrest Gump*. Laugh all you want, but they were all about overlooked people doing great things, and that gave me hope.

A couple of weeks later, I was at the promoter's place. He talked me through everything; ticket pricing strategies, different types of events, how to approach big named DJ's, everything. Club nights were popular but super competitive, and you could only attract 18+. With raves, though, you could go under 18s. More market, more margin.

Then he mentioned a venue.

It was a specific licensed location that held other rave-style parties all the time. One catch: it was also an outlaw bikie clubhouse.

Yep. One of those.

The kind of place where the rules are more like guidelines. Anyway, the party went perfectly and everyone had a great time.

We broke down the costs and worked out a promo strategy. To run the party, I'd need around $6,000–$7,000 plus a serious work ethic. But I was all in.

"You gonna do it?" he asked.

"Without a doubt."

At the time, the only things I owned were an old 1987 Mitsubishi Magna (maybe worth two grand if I was lucky), a Yamaha 1100 Virago motorbike (worth about five or six grand) that I'd worked a part-time job as a postie to purchase, a collection of DJ vinyl, and a wardrobe full of baggy jeans and rave shirts. That was it.

So I made the decision; sell the car and the bike, use the money to throw the party, then use the party profits to fund the deposit on a property. I figured I'd sort out another car later.

I came home and hit Mum with the announcement.

"Mum, guess what, I'm buying a property."

We hadn't even talked about it for over a month, so she was caught off guard.

"Oh really? Go on then..."

"Well... this might sound crazy in your world, but trust me, this is going to work."

I still laugh at the level of confidence/delusion I had at 18, but also, I admire the blind belief.

"So here's the plan," I told her, "I'm going to sell my car and my motorbike. Then I'm going to use the money to promote an underground rave party at a Bikie Clubhouse that runs other raves. I'll sell tickets, and I'll use the money from the event as my property deposit."

Her response was immediate.

"The hell you are!"

Dad walks into the room mid-sentence.

"What's going on?"

I explained the plan again. Same reaction.

He's losing it. She's losing it.

"You are NOT doing this."

"You are NOT selling your car."

"You are NOT selling your bike."

"You are NOT throwing a party with bikies."

Every objection you could think of, they threw at me. But this was one of those pivotal moments in life, one of those forks in the road.

If I'd backed down and said, "Yeah, fair enough, I won't do it," that would've been it. I know for a fact my life would've gone in a completely different direction. I wouldn't be where I am now.

I can say this without a shred of doubt: **That one moment, that decision to back myself despite their objections, changed the course of my life.**

Now look, I'm a parent now, so I get it. They were right to be worried. I was an 18-year-old selling off everything I owned to throw a *party* at a bikie clubhouse. I get the concern.

But I'm still incredibly proud of my 18-year-old self for looking them both in the eye and saying:

"You're wrong. This is going to work. And I'm doing it anyway."

The next day, I listed my car and my motorbike for sale.

"You're NOT bloody selling them!" Mum yelled.

But they were already mentally gone. The plan was in motion.

Within two weeks, both were sold. I paid for the venue, locked in the date, and started ticking off the to-do list.

I got a contact who could print tickets, so I had 1,500 printed and delivered. I had a mate who was good with graphic design and had experience with rave flyers, so he whipped up something cool and got me thousands of copies. Another mate had just started out in sound and lighting, and he offered to do the whole event for $500 if he could use it as a portfolio piece to help book future gigs. Legend.

Then I called and organised public liability insurance. Because even at 18, as rogue as this idea was, I wasn't silly, I knew I had to cover myself legally and do everything right.

Suddenly, it was real. I had organised a venue, flyers, tickets, sound, lighting, and insurance. I even had about two grand left over for booking DJs.

The promoter, who was a well-known DJ himself and had been helping me through the process, said he'd play for free. Absolute legend. I still owe him.

Then I contacted three of the biggest names in Sydney's rave scene. They took up most of the remaining $2k, but having four credible headliners made the whole thing feel legit.

I still had a bit of cash left, so I booked another few DJs who were known in the scene but not quite drawcards yet. The rest of the lineup would be filled by up-and-comers.

And here's where the strategy kicked in.

I had heaps of DJ mates, really good *bedroom banger* DJs, but most had only ever played house parties in front of 50–100 people. This was their chance to play to a real crowd, with real production, on a real stage.

So I gave them one job: **sell 20 tickets and you can play a set**.

Then I added a twist: the more tickets you sold, the better your time slot. The top seller played the peak set. The lowest seller opened the night.

I picked 10 DJs from different friend groups and gave them each a bundle of tickets. They hit the pavement like street-level promoters, all competing to climb the setlist ladder. I'd never seen such a motivated bunch of DJs in my life.

Most sold exactly 20, but the highest ticket seller sold 86.

In the meantime, every Thursday night, Friday night, Saturday night, I was attending club nights, raves, and house parties to hand out flyers and talk people into coming to my one-off event.

Everything was coming together beautifully.

So I thought.

Party day had finally arrived.

The clubhouse gave us access to start bumping in from 3pm. The party officially kicked off at 9pm and would run until 6am. That gave us six hours to transform a rough-and-ready clubhouse into a fully functioning rave venue.

I rocked up with my crew, absolutely buzzing and a little nervous. We started unloading gear, setting up lights, and arranging the space. But very quickly, two major problems surfaced, and I mean **major**.

First: the **speakers** the venue was providing? Completely cooked. Distorted sound, blown woofers, buzzing feedback. They were unusable. By this point it's 7pm on a Saturday, any equipment hire business is shut.

Second: **there was no stage**.

At first I thought, *surely this is a stitch-up*. But no, they'd just forgotten to mention that the stage was packed away out the back. Thankfully, we found it and got it assembled, but the speaker situation had me absolutely sweating.

With the clock ticking, I rang a mate in a state of panic, who was both DJing and planning to attend.

"Hey bro, I need a *huge* favour. I need you to go home, grab your full speaker setup, chuck it in the car and bring it to the venue, ASAP."

He was supposed to catch a train, but I told him he'd have to drive now. He didn't hesitate. Just said, "No worries, I'm on it." I owe him big time!

By now it was around 7:30pm. We were 90 minutes out from the doors opening, and I still didn't have a sound system that worked.

8:30pm rolls around. There's already a queue forming out front. People are buzzing, lining up, ready to party, and I'm inside pacing like a madman, knowing that the speakers still weren't working properly. We were getting desperate. We *had* to start letting people in at 9pm whether the sound was right or not.

At 9pm, we opened the doors.

We rigged up what we had and kicked things off with the first DJ on vinyl. The sound was tinny. No bass. It felt like we were throwing a rave through laptop speakers. But somehow, *somehow*, the crowd didn't seem to care. They were still dancing, still smiling.

At 9:10pm, my mate with the speaker setup arrived.

I bolted outside, grabbed one of the big speakers and the massive subwoofer out of his car, and ran it through the crowd, dodging bodies and gear as I went.

The moment I plugged that subwoofer in and the bass hit the room, it was like flicking a switch. The whole crowd **roared**.

You could feel it.

The place turned into a proper rave in seconds.

People were jumping. Cheering. The energy went through the roof. The DJ's face changed instantly, you could see the relief. Within five minutes, we had all three new speakers in, running perfectly.

Crisis averted. Party: activated.

And let me tell you, that night was electric.

Big-name DJs came up to me mid-party like, "Hey Shaw, how are you going man?" You could tell they were being friendly, hoping to get on future line-ups. Regardless, it was a cool feeling. Clubhouse members were patting me on the back, saying, "You've done a bloody good job with this, well done." Just regular partygoers coming up, eyes wide, telling me, "This is the best party I've ever been to."

I was walking around this grungy clubhouse, fluorescent wristbands everywhere, people vibing to hardstyle under strobe lights, and I just kept thinking, *we actually pulled this off.*

I still remember so many little details: the smell of the smoke machine, the click of vinyl between sets, the feel of that sticky floor under my shoes. It was a gritty, beautiful, chaotic success.

And most importantly?

I needed **180 people** to break even.

We had **over 900** through the doors at one point.

With ticket sales and door sales, I walked out of that event having raised enough money to comfortably pay my taxes and still have a healthy chunk left for a deposit on a property.

That money came home with me in the most professional, secure method imaginable: **a backpack full of cash**.

After packing down the event (which went well into the morning), the crew and I hit up Macca's. I finally got home around 11am.

Now obviously, I couldn't just walk in and say *"I told you so"* to Mum and Dad. That would've been way too easy, and not nearly as satisfying.

Instead, I put on this defeated look. Slumped shoulders. Blank stare. Head down.

I walked in and sat at the kitchen table.

Mum and Dad joined me, looking more concerned than ever. The silence was heavy. They were 100% certain the party had been a disaster and probably thinking *we warned him.*

Then I stood up, opened my backpack, flipped it upside down, and let a **storm of $10, $20 and $50 notes** spill out all over the table and kitchen.

"So," I said, "the party went really well. It's time to buy the property."

A couple of weeks after the party, I was driving around with Mum and Dad when we happened to pass an open home in Burwood.

Mum said, "Why don't we check this one out?"

I wasn't particularly interested, I still had my heart set on buying in Ryde, closer to where most of my mates lived. But I figured, *why not.* It's open, we're here, may as well.

We walked in, had a quick look around, and straight away I thought, *Alright... it's not Ryde, but it's close enough, and it's actually a way better apartment than anything I've seen in Ryde, and it's a lot cheaper.*

So, I bought it. Just like that.

I was 18 years old, and I said to the real estate agent, "I want to buy this place."

He sort of smiled like I was taking the piss. Until I pulled out the deposit, 0.25% of the purchase price, in actual cash and handed it to him on the spot.

What I didn't realise was that I should've probably had a pre-approval in place or even spoken with a bank about getting a loan. Or maybe had a solicitor review the contract. Or done any number of things adults do when they buy property.

But I wasn't an adult in the typical sense, I was a DJ with a dream, a backpack full of rave money, and a rapidly growing belief that anything was possible.

Contracts were signed. I had a 7-day cooling off period to sort out finance and get the building and pest done.

Now, here's the thing, it was the Christmas period. Public holidays, skeleton staff, slow responses everywhere. I had no idea what a mortgage broker was at the time, so I just walked into a major bank branch. Why that one? Because one of my mate's mums worked there.

Genius-level strategy.

I had a chat with one of their internal home loan guys and explained the situation.

He asked about my income, by this stage, I'd moved into a higher role and was earning around $45,000 a year. No debts, barely any expenses. Just a young bloke with a steady income and no baggage.

He punched some numbers into his computer, paused, then smiled and said: "Mate, I'll tell you something, you've broken two records for me today. First, you're the youngest person I've ever approved for a mortgage.

And second, this is the fastest loan I've ever seen get formally approved. The computer has given you the green light."

Just like that, I was buying a property.

Now, I've spent a fair chunk of this book talking about how I bought that first property because, honestly, that was the hardest part of the entire journey.

People don't realise it, but when it comes to building a property portfolio, getting the first one is often the biggest mountain to climb. It's like pushing a boulder up a hill, but once you're over the crest, the momentum kicks in and things start moving on their own.

Building a portfolio is 100% a marathon, not a sprint. But in the beginning, you do need these mad, crazy sprints, these *bursts* of wild energy, to get yourself into the race in the first place.

I promise you, there will be plenty of time where 'you' can sit around on your arse, but you first need to make sure the *market is working hard for you.*

If you can push yourself to that first property, and give the market a chance to work in your favour, it can absolutely change your life.

And that's what happened to me.

Between 2008 and 2009, the Sydney property market started to take off. Especially in Burwood. My little apartment that I bought for $270,000 jumped in value to around $550,000.

That's a **$280,000 gain.** Just sitting there. No renos, no flips, no genius strategy. The market just moved.

Let me ask you this: do you reckon I could have saved $280,000 working a 9-5 job?

Not a chance. That's a lot of Friday night DJ gigs and late-night Maccas runs.

It was around this time I first heard the word "equity" in a way that actually made sense. I'd seen it in bank ads, you know, those old-school ones where a bloke with a moustache goes, *"Equity maaate."* But it was always just a buzzword. Until then.

Here's how it clicked.

It was 2009. My best mate and I had just come back from a trip to Thailand. I was hooked. I loved the culture shock, the energy, the freedom. I wanted more.

So I started saving my hard earned money for another trip, this time to the US and Mexico. I was planning a proper bucket list tour: Spring Break in Cancun, nights out in New York, watching a boxing main event at the MGM Grand in Vegas and much more. The works.

That trip, those six or seven weeks, was another lightbulb moment. I met so many travellers who spoke about doing long stints around the world. And I thought, *That's what I want next.* A big one. Europe! UK visa. Backpacking. Living the dream.

The only problem?

I needed a big chunk of money to do it.

So I did what any logical person would do, I went back to the bank.

I spoke to one of those personal loan people, the kind that feel like they're just one cubicle away from the teller. I told her my situation.

"I want to travel Europe for a couple of years, but I don't know how I'm going to afford it."

She asked a few questions and then said, "Well, if we're being honest, we probably can't give you a loan if you're planning to quit your job, because that income is how we assess your ability to repay."

Damn. Makes sense.

Then she asked, "Do you own any assets?"

"Oh yeah," I said, "I've got a property."

Her whole tone shifted.

"Right, okay, let's explore that."

She typed in the address, pulled up the loan details and then said, "Well, it looks like you've got about $200,000 in equity sitting there. Do you want to use it?"

"Sorry, what exactly is *equity* again?"

She explained it's the difference between what your property's worth and what you still owe on the loan. If I sold the place tomorrow, the leftover money, after paying off the bank, would be mine. That's the equity.

"Okay, cool. Well... can I take out like $50,000?"

By this point the Loan to Value Ratio was so low that it was automatically accepted.

"No problem."

And just like that, *boom*, we were going to Europe.

At that time in my life, I made some questionable financial decisions. People thought I was a bit silly for doing it. From my perspective at the time (and I still echo that perspective today), I was going to spend two years living abroad, something not everyone gets to do, and I was funding it with a property I bought where the value increased without me doing anything.

Looking back, I was young, impulsive, and frankly, I was living my best crazy life without working too hard. There was no-one my age that I would swap lives with...but I think a fair few secretly would have swapped with me.

This just cemented it in my mind that property was a phenomenal investment vehicle for building wealth. I knew that once I was done living my 20s to the max, I was going to become a Property Investor.

I started preparing for a long stint overseas. This time I was going with a girlfriend at the time, and we were planning to be away for a year or two.

We got over there, and for the first three months, we travelled together.

We did some of the big cities, London, Berlin, Rome, Barcelona. But after about three months, we broke up. In Paris, of all places. Unplanned, but pretty funny when you think about it.

It was one of those awkward, emotionally cooked breakups where I didn't really know what to do next, so I continued the trip on my own.

That's when the real adventure started.

I travelled to over 40 new countries, *solo*. I did use my UK visa, but after two months working in a pub, earning next to nothing and spending more than I earned to have a good time, I sat down and ran the numbers. It was actually cheaper for me to quit my London job and travel through Eastern Europe than it was to live and work in London.

So that's exactly what I did.

I quit my job the next day and flew to Poland.

From there, I bounced around: Hungary, Slovakia, Croatia, Romania, Latvia, Estonia, you name it. I went full backpacker mode. Shoestring budget, night buses, hostels, cans of beer on trains, you name it. But I loved every second of it.

Meanwhile, back in Australia, my Sydney apartment just kept going up in value. I hadn't touched it. I wasn't working. I wasn't doing anything. But that property was still increasing in value while I was out in Europe living life.

I returned home in 2013, and I was absolutely wrecked, in a good way. I felt like I had properly lived. I had done the travel thing. Ticked the boxes. Worn out the party life. So I was thinking... alright, that's probably it for me.

I went to the bank to get another equity release. I wanted to buy another property straight away & also do some renovations to my Sydney apartment. At the time, it was a "head down, bum up" mentality, time to take life a bit more seriously. I completed a Diploma & Advanced Diploma of Financial Planning and am ready to take on the corporate world.

But then I was living with one of my best mates and telling him all my crazy travel adventures and he decided he wanted to do it also. Within a couple of months and plenty of beers, he talked me into doing another trip with him.

We decided to do another big Europe stint and also South America.

This trip was even more fun because I wasn't working or stressing about anything. I wasn't trying to party as hard as before, either, I was starting to slow down a bit (I had my moments haha). I'd had my big club nights, the crazy hostel stories, the sunrise-after-no-sleep kind of adventures.

But I still loved being on the road. Seeing the world. Eating street food. Drinking cheap beers in old towns. Getting lost on purpose. I especially loved going to places that weren't on the map and finding people who didn't speak a word of English.

That for me is travelling.

When you're trying to find somewhere to sleep and food to eat and no-one speaks English and you're forced to try to communicate in their language. The best!

But while I was overseas this time, I started having some realisations.

I was about 27 or 28, and decided I was over partying. Not just for now... like, properly done. I'd almost hit my *life quota* of partying. The candles were well and truly burned at both ends.

Like, am I just going to be a lifelong partygoer? Or am I going to take this property investing thing seriously and build a future?

I got back home and had a look at the property market. I couldn't believe what had happened to Sydney.

Houses that I looked at in 2012 for $650,000, and seriously considered buying, were now going for $1.5 million. Same house, same suburb, just a few years later.

Melbourne had already passed a million bucks in plenty of places too.

I was blown away.

I remember having chats with my mates and work colleagues, and they'd be like, "Yeah bro, it's f**ked. Guess we're not buying a house."

But I had a different take.

I'm not raising my future family in an apartment.

I grew up on a farm and then later on a 1,200 sqm block. My kids were going to have the same kind of space. And if I couldn't afford to do that in Sydney or Melbourne, then I was going to find a place that I could.

And that's when I started to seriously look at **Brisbane**.

I did a proper deep dive, looked at data, spoke to locals, asked my Brisbane mates about new infrastructure, upcoming shopping centres, schools, parks, public transport upgrades, the whole lot. Visited Brisbane many times.

Every single arrow pointed to North Lakes in the Moreton Bay Region.

Not only that, but on a personal level, I'm a keen golfer, and I race motorbikes. Within 10 minutes of North Lakes, I had Lakeside Park for racing and a championship golf course right in town. It was basically built for me.

That was it. I was sold.

I made the decision to buy in North Lakes for $400,000.

I didn't know if it was going to boom the same way Sydney and Melbourne had... but I had a good feeling. Worst case, I'd own a house I liked in a place I could see myself living. Best case, it grows like crazy and sets me up for the next level.

Now, how did I buy it?

Well, this time, I went to a **Mortgage Broker**. I'd never used one before, but I'd heard they were helpful. We refinanced the Sydney apartment, factored in the expected rental income from both properties, and used the equity sitting in that first place to fund the new one.

I didn't have to do anything extra. The whole process was straightforward. It honestly blew my mind how easy it was compared to buying the first property.

I called up a local Property Manager, and they got tenants into the North Lakes house within a few weeks. Just like that, I was earning rent, my mortgage was covered, and I officially owned two properties.

I remember having a beer one night to celebrate and thinking, *more people need to know how easy it is to buy a second property.* Like, seriously. If you already own one, and the market's done a bit of work for you, the second one can practically fall into your lap.

And I couldn't help but think... if this is how easy it is to get number two, I can only imagine how easy number 3, 4 and 5 will be.

I waited about 12 months. The market had moved again. I'd gotten another promotion at work and my salary had increased. So I went back to the same Mortgage Broker and asked the question, *Can I buy another property?*

Apparently, that's called your "borrowing capacity." (I didn't know all the proper terms at the time, I just knew I wanted another one.)

He ran the numbers and came back with, "Yep, you could spend up to $500,000 on the next one."

I was keen. I thought, *If Brisbane's going to boom, and I reckon it will, then having two properties there would be way better than just one.*

This time, someone told me I should speak with a Buyers Agent. I was a bit sceptical at first, I mean, I'd already bought two places on my own. I thought, *Surely I can just do this myself.*

But I was curious enough to meet with one.

The Buyers Agent had a financial planning background, and I liked that. He didn't just talk hype, he showed me data. He talked about macro trends, suburb-level insights, market drivers, historical growth, migration data, infrastructure pipelines, and economic fundamentals.

But more importantly, he had serious results to back it all up.

After understanding my goals, he presented me with an off-market property. No public listing, no bidding war, no stress. It was a two-storey townhouse, close to Brisbane CBD. Three good-sized bedrooms, two bathrooms, a two-car lock-up garage.

The layout was great and it had rental appeal. The numbers more than stacked up.

But then he showed me why it stacked up, and that's when my mind changed about Buyers Agents forever.

He walked me through everything:

- Suburb selection criteria
- Labour market stats
- Population growth projections
- Gentrification trends
- Upcoming infrastructure spending
- Vacancy rates and rental yield data
- Days on market
- Auction clearance rates
- Median prices compared to surrounding areas
- Flood and fire risk mapping
- Zoning laws
- Supply constraints

» Owner-occupier ratios
» Layout appeal for PPR tenants
» Maintenance forecasts
» Title info and strata details

I'd never seen this level of **granularity** before.

I was used to checking out open homes, chatting with real estate agents, trusting my gut, asking friends that lived in the area and trying not to get sucked into bidding wars. I thought that was how you bought property.

But this was different. It was **data-driven**. Emotionless. Strategic. And, off-market.

I learned more in that one meeting with the Buyers Agent than I had in years of doing it on my own. And it changed the way I approached property forever.

While all this was going on, I was still working in **insurance**. At this point, my LinkedIn said I'd been in the industry for about 15 years (less 4 years travelling, shhh).

I'd climbed the ladder. Started in the mailroom. Then case management. Then more senior roles. Eventually, I became a **Senior Product Manager**, overseeing product development and the financial performance of a major insurer. Later, I became one of the top **Business Development Managers** in another.

I did all the right things. I completed my **Financial Planning qualifications**, knocked out a **Masters of Business Administration (MBA)**, and built a resume that looked great on paper. My LinkedIn profile was super professional.

If I'd stayed in that world, I was well on track to make $250,000+ a year, easy. Probably more by the time you're reading this book.

But I wasn't fulfilled. Something inside me always knew I was meant for more and I wasn't going to find it in insurance. I had this quiet voice in my head that kept saying: *You're settling.*

That job, that industry, it was the matrix. Normal to everyone else, but not to me. I'd already tasted freedom. I'd seen the world. I'd used property to fund my life. I knew there was another way to live.

And then something eventually forced me to make a change, and it came in the form of a few big, honest conversations.

In 2019, my girlfriend at the time, now my wife, Sarah, and I started seriously talking about our future. We both wanted to get married, have kids, and do all the old-school stuff that you don't really think about when you're 24 and living out of a backpack.

And those conversations made me take a hard look at my lifestyle.

I was working a standard 9-5 job, Monday to Friday. But let's be real, it wasn't just 9-5.

I'd wake up around 6:30am, get ready, sometimes try to squeeze in a gym session, commute to work, sit in traffic... and by the time I got home, it was often 6:30 or 7pm. That's not a 9-5. That's your whole day gone.

And Monday to Friday, that's 70% of your life.

So I started asking the question: *When am I actually going to be a Dad?*

Kids wake up early, and they go to bed around 6–7pm. So if I'm gone in the morning and not back in time for bed, *when do I even see them?*

It made me think about my own Dad. He left for work before we woke up. Got home late. Some nights he was back in time for dinner, some nights we were already in bed. He did what he had to do for the family, and I'll always respect him for that, but I knew I didn't want the same setup.

And it's not the 80s or 90s anymore. We live in the 2020s now. You can work from home. You can build businesses online. There are so many ways to create income that don't involve sacrificing time with your kids.

Sarah and I had long conversations about it. I told her I wanted to try something different. I didn't want to spend the next 20 years climbing the insurance corporate ladder and only seeing my kids on weekends.

She backed me completely.

She said, "You know what? Go for it. Leave insurance now. Take the risk now while we're young. Try something for a couple of years. I know you'll make it work. But if for whatever reason, it doesn't work, insurance will always be there."

I'll never forget that support. It meant everything.

Around that same time, there were redundancies happening in the company. People in our department were being quietly shortlisted, and the tension was pretty heavy. So much for the "safe job, 9-5 life."

So I picked up the phone and called my manager.

I said, "Hey, I've had a think about everything, and if someone in our team needs to go... I won't be upset if it's me."

A few months went by while they worked it all out. I won't go into too much detail about what happened behind the scenes, but let's just say, *they could've saved some money* by letting me go earlier than they did.

And then it happened.

March 6th, 2020.

My last day in the insurance industry.

Fifteen years. Done.

It was one of the scariest days of my life.

I was walking away from **close to $200,000 a year** in income, to go and try something completely unknown. I'd never done anything outside of insurance. This was the first proper leap into the unknown.

But I had a plan.

I'd already lined up a role as a **Business Development Manager** for a Strategic HR company. It was a great company, doing amazing work in their space. I was excited. That job was supposed to start on **March 30th, 2020**.

But you can probably guess what happened next.

Between **March 6th and March 30th**, the whole world went sideways.

COVID lockdowns hit Australia.

Just like that, the job was gone. The world shut down. Hiring froze. Everyone panicked.

So here I am, jobless. Depressed by the way my corporate exit was handled. Property tenants moving out. Rent not coming in. Markets in freefall. And that voice in my head that said, *You're meant for more*?

It had gone pretty bloody quiet.

For a while, I was in a really dark place.

Financial stress was immediate. Opportunities vanished. I felt like I had made the biggest mistake of my life. There were some horrible thoughts going through my head.

But I had two choices: dwell in it, or level up.

So I chose to double down.

I went all in on study. If I couldn't make money, I'd invest in knowledge. I started reading property books, attending webinars, listening to podcasts, anything I could get my hands on.

Eventually, I landed a work-from-home job with a Financial Services company that specialised in using property (along with shares and business) as a vehicle to build long-term wealth for clients.

And this job? It opened up a whole new world for me.

I was working closely with one of Australia's leading Wealth Coaches, and the level of knowledge I gained in that time absolutely eclipsed anything I'd learned through Financial Planning or even my MBA.

It also made me question the validity of higher education... but let's not get into that.

I learned about:

» Tax structuring
» Asset protection
» Diversification
» Long-term strategy
» Intergenerational wealth

And most importantly, how to build a portfolio without relying on active income.

And while all that was happening, the property market went ballistic.

COVID sparked a boom, and my portfolio jumped by more than $1 million in two years.

Interest rates hit record lows. Everyone said the market was going to crash... but it didn't. It exploded. The money printer went brrrrrr, and property values surged.

And with all the knowledge I'd gained, I felt ready to buy again.

This time, I went West.

Perth.

Now, keep in mind, this was 2022. We were in the peak of Covid lockdowns. The media was screaming *doom and gloom*. Everyone was saying the market was cooked, property "experts" on TV saying it's a questionable time to buy, property was overpriced, interest rates were going to skyrocket, and we were heading into a full-blown crash.

But if there's one thing I'd learned by now, it's this:

"There is always a market about to boom."

Even if the national headlines are all negative, there's always a *local* market, or even a suburb within a market, that's primed for growth.

And based on the data I was looking at, southern Perth was the area.

Not emotionally. Not because I had mates over there. Not because it looked good on Instagram. But because the numbers told me it was the right move.

So I lined up another Buyers Agent, this time someone who really understood *Perth,* lived and breathed that market, and had a track record of spotting good deals.

We ended up buying a house for **$418,000.**

It was cash flow positive from day one, rented out for **$750 a week** straight off the bat. That's a wild rental yield, especially compared to what was happening in other cities at the time.

A $2million property in Sydney could be rented for not much more than $750 p/week.

It didn't cost me a cent out of pocket. My other properties covered everything. I just made a few calls, filled out some forms, and suddenly, I had a fourth property, making money and building wealth in the background.

And here's the kicker...

By **2024**, that $418,000 property was worth **$730,000**.

That's over **$300,000** in growth... in two years... without me having to lift a finger. No renos. No major maintenance costs. Just the right market, at the right time, with the right people helping me.

And it all came from understanding this one core lesson:

"The media doesn't know what the hell it's talking about."

The news is there to get clicks and make you emotional, not to help you build wealth. Most people make property decisions based on emotion or fear. But real investors? They make them based on data.

So when all the noise said, "Now's a terrible time to buy," I knew that was the exact moment to double down.

And it worked.

This is why I love property.

Tell me another investment vehicle where you can:

- Make a few phone calls
- Sign a few documents
- Use other people's money (the bank's and your tenants')

...and end up with an asset that increases in value by **$300,000** in two years... *without costing you a single cent out of pocket.*

That's what property can do.

Now don't get me wrong, I'm not saying property is the only way to build wealth. I diversify. I've got other investments in shares, super, and business too. I encourage everyone to seek out proper, personal financial advice that suits their situation.

But property? It's been the foundation of everything I've built.

And if you zoom out and look at Australian history; through recessions, GFCs, Royal Commissions, housing affordability crises, rate rises, and pandemics, property has consistently gone up. And if you strip away the politics, the headlines, the fear, and the media hype... there are two things that keep driving property values up in this country: **Inflation**, and **Immigration.**

Whether we like it or not, those two forces aren't slowing down anytime soon.

And they're both pushing up the long-term value of Australian real estate.

Now, it's **2025.**

I'm **36 years old**, and as I'm writing this, we're about four weeks away from settling on our dream home, a beautiful acreage property that ticks every single box we could've imagined.

It's got the open space I dreamed about as a kid. It's ten minutes from the boat ramp, twelve minutes from the beach, fourteen minutes from one of Brisbane's best golf courses, and twenty-four minutes from the 4WD beach access, perfect for camping trips with the kids.

And the best part?

The house is debt-free.

No mortgage. No repayments. Just complete ownership of the kind of lifestyle property most people assume they'll only afford in retirement, if ever.

If you consider my entire story, from where I started, through all the chaos, the risk, the travel, the parties, the ups and downs, tell me a way you can, leave school with no qualifications, have two **"once in a lifetime"** two year career breaks to spend your 20s travelling to 70+ countries, and still end up at 37 years old in your dream home with no debt...

...other than property?

And I don't say that to brag. I say that to prove what's possible.

My kids are now 3 years old and a newborn. I'm at home. I'm present. I get to be the Dad I always wanted to be, the kind who's actually there. Not just for the big milestones, but for the small moments too. School drop-offs. Morning routines. Afternoon park runs. Midday tickle fights. Watching them grow, day by day, not just catching up on weekends.

I get to have a hands-on influence in their lives, not just financially, but emotionally, mentally, and spiritually. I get to be the Dad who's actually *around*, not the one who's always "too busy" or "too tired" or "still at work."

And that's why I wrote this book.

Because the system we're all taught to follow, school, uni, job, climb the ladder, retire at 65, doesn't guarantee this kind of life. In fact, it pretty much guarantees the opposite.

I've met hundreds of people now who followed that path to the letter and still feel trapped. They've done everything "right," but have nothing to show for it except a HECS debt, a mortgage they'll die with, and a boss who replaces them with a cheaper version the second they ask for flexibility.

And then they wonder why they feel stuck. The truth is, you don't have to do it that way. There are other paths.

And I'm not special. I didn't have wealthy parents or insider knowledge. I didn't inherit anything. I wasn't given the golden ticket. I just backed myself.

I made bold moves and I learned through experience. I failed forward and I worked when I had to and I played harder when I could. And I made sure that every dollar I earned did something useful behind the scenes like buying me freedom.

That's what property did for me.

And if I can do it, *so can you.*

Why You Can Do This Too

Now, you might be sitting there thinking, "Yeah cool story mate, but that was then... things are different now."

And I get it, it *feels* harder now. Everything costs more. Wages haven't exactly skyrocketed. The media keeps telling you property's unaffordable, the market's cooked, interest rates are up, and unless your parents gave you a $200k head start, you've got no chance.

But I'm telling you right now, that's just not true.

If you strip away all the noise and doom-and-gloom headlines, the reality is... we've never lived in a better time to build real wealth.

In fact, it's never been easier to become a millionaire in Australia than it is today, and I say that with full conviction.

With the amount of information, access to finance, free tools, online support, education, and with more people than ever pushing against the old system, there is no excuse anymore.

You don't need to be rich. You don't need to be an expert. You don't need to be "lucky."

You just need to make a few good quality decisions, and then actually back them with action.

That's it. A Mentor once told me:

"You are about 3–4 good decisions away from achieving everything you've ever wanted financially."

Let that sink in. Not 50. Not 100. Just a few.

For most people, it's this simple:

Buy one quality investment property that doesn't kill your cashflow

Learn about equity and how to safely use it

Work with people who understand the game better than you do

And repeat it two or three times with a long-term mindset

That's it.

You don't need ten properties. You don't need to flip houses. You don't need to renovate, become a developer, or start a YouTube channel teaching property. You just need a small, well-built portfolio of the right assets in the right locations, and time will do the heavy lifting for you.

And the crazy thing is...

This doesn't take a decade to start feeling. You don't need to wait until retirement.

You can feel it after your second or third deal. That shift. That momentum. That feeling of *"Hang on a second... I'm actually building something here."*

And from there, every smart decision just compounds.

I've said it before, but I'll say it again: I wasn't born into this. I didn't know anything about finance when I started. I wasn't naturally disciplined. I didn't even know what the job I applied for was. I was just a young bloke who wanted freedom and found a way to make it happen.

I partied. I travelled. I made mistakes. I got it wrong plenty of times.

But I started early, and I stayed in the game. That's it.

So if you're reading this and wondering if this is still possible for *you*, let me be crystal clear:

Yes. It is.

And if you've read this far, you're already ahead of 90% of people.

Don't let the headlines scare you.

Don't wait for the "perfect" time.

And don't let fear of stuffing it up stop you, because even if you don't nail it the first time, you're still going to be ahead of everyone else who never even tried.

Start with one good property. Let the market do its thing. Let time do its thing. And let that first deal become the launchpad for the rest of your life.

It worked for me. It's worked for thousands of others. And if you stick around, I'll show you how it can work for you too.

Part 1: The Property Mindset

The Great Lie of the 9-5

Let's talk about the 9–5. Because for most people, that's the goal, right? Finish school, get a job, stick with it, climb the ladder, get a couple of pay rises, maybe a house, and if you're lucky, retire before your knees give out.

But if we're being honest, it's a bit of a stitch-up, isn't it?

It's sold to us as "security"... but what it actually becomes for most people is a trap.

A really well-decorated, socially accepted, financial trap that's hard to spot until you're already in too deep.

At first, it's exciting.

You're earning more than you ever have before. You upgrade the car, rent a nicer place, maybe even buy something. You start to feel like you've made it.

But before long, the promotions slow down, the cost of living catches up, and now you *need* that income just to survive.

And that's when it starts to feel like golden handcuffs.

Because you're not in love with your job, but you can't walk away either.

The money's *too good to quit*, but not good enough to change your life.

You're stuck in this weird middle ground, where your life looks "successful" from the outside, but inside, something's missing.

And here's the thing, it's not just you. That's the system.

The 9–5 was never designed to make you free, it was designed to keep you showing up.

It keeps you just happy enough to not rock the boat, and just tired enough to never build something of your own.

And I'll tell you the exact moment I knew I had to get out...

It was a bloke I used to work with, we'll call him *Dave*.

Dave started working in insurance when he was 17 years old. Same industry. Same type of job. And after nearly 50 years, he finally retired. Sixty-five years old, walking out the door on his last day, people clapping, handing him a card, giving him one of those glass trophies no one ever keeps.

"Congratulations on an amazing career," they all said. "What a legacy," they said.

But I'll never forget the look in his eyes.

He smiled, yeah. He said all the right things. But you could see it, deep down, behind the polite smile and handshake. There were regrets. A lot of them.

You could see the passion that never got expressed. The business that never got started. The ideas that never left the notebook. The skills the world never got to see. A lifetime of *maybe next year* moments that ran out of years.

That moment hit me like a truck. Because I saw myself in him, and I thought, *"If I don't make a move soon, that's going to be me."*

I was already 15 years deep in insurance at that point. Senior role. Decent money. Good title. All the right boxes ticked. But inside, I was already drifting into someone I didn't want to become. I was on the path to applause, not freedom. And that's when I knew, I had to pull the pin and if I didn't change something now, I'd wake up at 65 wondering where my life went.

That's the great lie of the 9–5.

It feels safe. It looks safe. But it costs you more than you think.

It costs you your time, energy, dreams, your kids' childhood, your creativity, your actual *life*, while you spend your best years building someone else's. And worst of all, it convinces you that there's no other way. But there is. I promise you there is. I'm not saying quit your job tomorrow and move to Bali. But I am saying, have a plan. Start building something *now* so you don't get stuck later. Use your job to fund your freedom, not your retirement party. Because the earlier you see the trap, the sooner you can start working your way out of it.

You are 3–4 good decisions away from changing your entire financial life.

You just need to be honest with yourself about whether the path you're on is taking you where you actually want to go. And if it's not, you've got two options: Ignore it... or do something about it. I chose the second one and it changed everything.

Millennials & Gen Z: The Wake-Up Call

Let's not sugarcoat it, Millennials and Gen Z have been dealt a very different hand compared to previous generations.

We've grown up through:

- Two global recessions
- A once-in-a-lifetime pandemic
- Skyrocketing property prices
- Wages that haven't kept up
- A cost of living crisis

And more contradictory financial advice than any generation before us.

We're the most *educated* generation, but also the most *debt-loaded.* We're told to save, but punished with inflation. Told to buy property, but priced out of our own cities. Told to invest, but warned about risk. Told to follow our passion, but scolded for not being "realistic."

And most of us grew up hearing some variation of the same 1950s financial advice:

"Work hard. Get a good job. Buy a house. Pay it off. Retire."

Sorry, but that's not a strategy anymore, that's a pipe dream.

In 2025, the rules of the game have changed. You can't rely on what your parents did, because that world doesn't exist anymore.

Their house cost $60k. Your coffee costs $7.

Their interest rates were high, yeah, but the loan amounts were tiny. They could pay off a mortgage on one income. They weren't drowning in HECS debt. Childcare didn't cost a second salary. And let's be honest no one was asking them to figure out crypto, AI, side hustles and personal branding at the same time just to get ahead.

So let me hit you with something direct: This generation has it harder (in some ways), but it also has *more* opportunity than any generation before it.

You just need to see through the noise.

Because while most people are *talking* about how hard things are... some people are out there doing something about it.

I've seen it firsthand. I've got mates, same age, same background, similar jobs, and yet we're in completely different places in life. Not because I'm smarter. Not because I had more money. But because at some point, I made a different decision.

I remember having conversations back in 2016–2017. Everyone was saying:

> "There's no point, property's cooked."
>
> "We're never buying a house."
>
> "May as well just rent forever."
>
> "Brisbane won't grow like Sydney or Melbourne."

But instead of joining in on the whinging, I went all in on Brisbane.

I looked at the data. I looked at where the infrastructure was going, the population growth, the new developments, the migration patterns, affordability, lifestyle drivers, and I backed myself. Then, a few years later, the same conversation came up again.

> "It's over now."
>
> "There's no money left in property."
>
> "It's a bubble."

That time, I went all in on Perth.

Both plays worked out. Really well. Because I wasn't following headlines, I was following strategy.

And that's what this generation needs to understand:

There is always a market about to move. There is always opportunity. There is always a way forward. But you won't find it in your parents' playbook.

Wealth creation in 2025 doesn't come from just working hard and hoping. It comes from thinking differently. Being willing to learn. Asking better questions. Taking calculated risks. And backing yourself when everyone else is playing it safe.

You don't need to be rich to get started. You don't need to know everything. You just need to stop waiting for perfect conditions and start making progress.

Because while some people are spending their 20s and 30s building portfolios, businesses and options, others are stuck complaining about how it's all too hard, while doing nothing about it.

And 10 years from now?

Those same people will be shaking their heads saying:

> "If only I bought when it was still affordable."
>
> "I remember when Brisbane was cheap."
>
> "I nearly bought in Perth but didn't."

It's just like those videos you see popping up of people from the 1960's saying *"land has gone up to $1,500, it's just overly inflated prices now and I don't understand how people can buy it anymore."*

Same mentality, same problem, different decade, different price.

The only difference between those people and the ones who did, is action. As the saying goes, "some people will find excuses and others will find a way."

Stop making excuses, and find a way!

You don't need ten properties. You don't need to be the next property mogul.

But you do need to stop looking at this like it's all rigged against you.

Because yes, things are harder, but the tools we have now? Insane.

You can analyse markets from your phone, access experts for free on YouTube, build a personal brand with zero dollars, and invest with far less capital than ever before.

So here's your wake-up call:

The opportunity is still out there! The market will keep moving with or without you. The choice is yours, play the game differently, or be left wondering why you didn't.

Why Now Is the Best Time in History to Build Wealth

Adversity is a privilege.
Adversity can breed victims, or it can breed heroes.

People love comparing today's challenges to how "easy" our parents supposedly had it. You've heard it before: *"My parents bought a house in Sydney for $250,000" or "...my Grandparents bought for $60,000," "...and now it's worth $2 million.*

And sure, I get it. I would've loved to snap up a 5-bedroom acreage 10 minutes from the beach in Sydney too. That sounds great. But let's be real, that's not a reasonable expectation anymore. The game has changed. But more importantly, the *city* has changed. The *world* has changed.

Let's break it down.

Then vs Now: Sydney's Global Evolution

Back in the 60s, 70s, and 80s, Sydney was a nice place to live, but it wasn't exactly a global powerhouse. The population was around 2-2.5 million. Our infrastructure? Pretty rough. Patchy train lines, barely any decent highways, a couple of stadiums and that's about it. A lot of people didn't even have proper driveways.

The economy was mostly blue collar, manufacturing, trades, labouring jobs. Hard-working Aussies doing their bit to build this great place we know today. But there weren't a lot of high-income opportunities. Immigration was low and sustainable. International investment was almost non-existent. Property prices moved slowly. There was no real pressure on land. Nothing to force a market to take off.

To put it simply, your parents didn't buy in a world-class city. They bought in a quiet, developing, faraway outpost that just happened to become a global icon over time.

I grew up on a farm in Sydney. That's gone now. The areas surrounding it are all subdivided, paved over, replaced with driveways, townhouses, and new suburbs. The world found us, and everything changed.

Sydney Today: One of the Top 7 Cities in the World

Fast forward to 2025 and you're living in a completely different Sydney.

We've got a population over 5.3 million, and that's still growing fast with unsustainable levels of immigration. We've got international airports, modern metros, world-class hospitals, and skyline-defining architecture.

We've got one of the highest global rankings in terms of liveability, safety, and economic resilience.

We're leaders in tech, finance, education, healthcare and green innovation. And we're now home to some of the biggest annual events on Earth; F1, MotoGP, Australian Open, Sydney Mardi Gras, Vivid Sydney, even global UFC and boxing cards. We went from a quiet harbour town to a city that people dream of visiting. Our Sydney New Years Fireworks display is the *most watched* fireworks display worldwide. That's a massive shift.

You know when you travel and see clocks on a wall showing global time zones? They used to say "New York, London, Tokyo, Paris..." now they say SYDNEY. That wasn't happening when your parents were driving down a dirt road to get to their fibro house after a 10-hour shift.

So What Does That Mean for You?

It means if you're out there trying to buy your *first ever home* in one of the top 7 cities on Earth, you've got to shift your perspective.

Your parents didn't do that. They didn't aim for a global powerhouse, they just bought where they could afford. And *because* they did that, they caught the wave when the market moved, and now they look like geniuses. And the reason they most likely can't help you in 2025, is because they can't properly articulate *'how'* they actually got wealthy. They weren't diversified. Their strategy wasn't on point. It just happened.

So maybe the smart move today is to buy in the next version of Sydney.

The cities that are still affordable. Still developing. Still flying under the radar. Places like Perth, Adelaide, Hobart, Brisbane, where the fundamentals are sound and the future is bright. Once they're all build up, it'll be sub-cities blowing up. In the 80's, Wollongong & Newcastle were less than desirable places to live. Now they're great sort after places to live. Plenty of work & starting to become super expensive. This is how it works. Eventually some country bumpkin town that's not on your radar will be selling for $1mil and you'll still be twiddling your thumbs saying *"I want to buy where my parents raised me."*

Get in early, build equity, and leverage up over time.

If your goal is to one day own your dream home in Sydney, maybe your first property isn't your forever property, maybe it's the launchpad.

Why It's Actually Easier Now Than Ever

Now I know some people reading this are still thinking, "Yeah, but it's just so hard these days."

Alright, let's look at that properly.

- » **Government Assistance:** First Home Buyer grants, shared equity schemes, 5% deposit loans with no LMI, stamp duty exemptions, your parents didn't have any of that.
- » **Mortgage Brokers:** Back then you had one bank. Today you've got access to 50 lenders and experts who know how to get you finance that suits your situation.
- » **Buyers Agents:** You don't have to guess anymore. You can pay a professional who literally runs the data, checks growth drivers, compares supply/demand curves and helps you buy off-market, smarter.

- **Knowledge is everywhere:** You can learn about property investing from podcasts, YouTube, courses, even TikTok. Education is no longer reserved for the wealthy.
- **You can invest remotely:** You don't even need to live in the city you invest in anymore. Buy a place in Brisbane or Perth while living in Sydney, it's all doable.

Yes, Sydney is expensive.

Yes, the cost of living is up.

Yes, there's noise in the media.

But if you zoom out and think long-term, there has never been a more supported, connected, and opportunity-rich time to build wealth.

You can:

- Use the bank's money (finance)
- Use the tenant's money (rent)
- Rely on capital growth to do the heavy lifting
- And start with as little as 5% deposit in some cases

And if you get that first property right, with the right fundamentals, you could double your money in five years and use that equity to keep moving up the ladder.

"You are only 3–4 good decisions away from achieving everything you've ever wanted financially." I really need you to remember that.

So stop focusing on what you *can't* do. Start asking what you *can*. Because right now, the opportunities are there. And they're wide open.

Scarcity vs Abundance: Rewriting the Script

Most of us were raised on a **scarcity mindset**, even if we didn't know it at the time. You probably heard things like:

> "Money doesn't grow on trees."
>
> "We can't afford that."
>
> "You've got to play it safe."
>
> "People like us don't live like that."

These are the little sentences that become the script playing in the background of your life. And if you don't pause and rewrite that script, it'll run the whole show, and not in your favour.

I don't say this to blame anyone. Most of our parents were doing the best they could with what they had. They grew up in a time of high interest rates, low financial education, and limited access to tools like we have now. But the world has changed, and if your mindset hasn't, it's time to update the software.

Scarcity Thinking Keeps You Stuck

Here's what a **scarcity mindset** sounds like in 2025:

> "All the good suburbs are gone."
>
> "I'll never be able to afford a house."
>
> "It's too risky to invest."
>
> "What if it doesn't work?"
>
> "You really need to play it safe, when we first bought our house we had interest rates up to 19%."

Sound familiar?

Scarcity thinking keeps you small. It tells you to shrink, delay, protect, wait for the perfect time. And guess what? That "perfect time" never comes. While you're sitting around waiting, someone else, maybe with less income, less knowledge, and less talent, has gone ahead and bought two properties and is already looking at their third.

That's not because they're lucky. It's because they see the world through abundance, not limitation.

Abundance is a Lens, Not a Lottery

Abundance doesn't mean pretending things are easy. It means knowing there's always a way forward.

It's choosing to believe:

> "If I don't know how to do this, I can learn."
>
> "If I don't have the money yet, I can figure out how to get it."
>
> "There's always another suburb, another opportunity, another run in the market."
>
> "There is more than enough success to go around, and I can have my share."

Abundance isn't fluff. It's not about manifesting on a vision board and hoping someone hands you a Ferrari. It's a mindset that allows you to move, act, and grow even when conditions aren't perfect, because they rarely are.

Rewriting the Script: From "I Can't" to "How Can I?"

The truth is, most people don't need to win the lotto or marry a millionaire, they just need to **ask better questions**.

Instead of saying "I can't afford a property," ask: "Where in Australia can I afford a property that's likely to grow?"

Instead of saying "I don't know how to invest," ask: "Who can I learn from who's already doing this successfully?"

Instead of saying "I could never retire early," ask: "What would I need to do in the next 5–10 years to make that possible?"

It's these little mindset shifts, done consistently, that change the trajectory of your life.

Scarcity Was a Survival Tool. Abundance Builds Empires.

Scarcity served a purpose, it helped your grandparents survive post-war years, recessions, and uncertainty. But this isn't 1952 anymore.

You're living in an age of:

- Low-deposit finance options
- Accessible education at your fingertips
- Government incentives
- Open property markets
- Remote investing
- Digital businesses you can start with your phone

If you're in Australia in 2025, you've already won the postcode lottery. The question is: what are you doing with it?

Most people underestimate how much power they have to change their circumstances. They live on autopilot, recycling old beliefs, old patterns, and old fears.

But that's not you. You wouldn't be reading this if you weren't ready to make a shift.

So here's your script from now on:

> ***There's always a way.***
> ***There's always more to learn.***
> ***There's always another opportunity.***
>
> *And if I'm willing to move, adapt, and take action,*
> ***wealth is within reach.***

Rewriting your mindset is the first property you should own. Once that's done, the rest becomes a lot easier.

The Cost of Doing Nothing

Most people think doing nothing is safe. They think *"I'll just wait a little longer,"* or *"Now's not the right time,"* or the classic, *"I'll do something about it when things calm down."*

Sometimes there's a good reason, but it's mostly because of "Loss Aversion Bias" whereas human beings typically place twice the mental energy and attention on what could go wrong, instead of what could go well.

But here's the thing, doing nothing might be the most expensive decision you ever make.

You don't get billed for inaction upfront. There's no invoice in the mail that says "Hey mate, just letting you know this 2 years of hesitation cost you $164,000 in capital growth." But you *do* pay, eventually. And usually, it's way more than you ever expected.

Let's say you were looking at a $500k property in Brisbane in 2020 and said *"eh, maybe next year."* Fast forward to 2025... that property is now worth $980k. You didn't save money by waiting. You lost $480,000.

Now factor in that you could've been:

- » Using the rental income to pay down debt
- » Claiming tax deductions
- » Building equity
- » And using that equity to buy your *second* property by now
- » Doing nothing just costs you the entire ladder.

Markets don't wait for you. They don't freeze just because you haven't made a decision yet. They keep rolling, with or without you.

People who bought in Perth in 2022 while everyone else was saying "it's cooked" they're laughing now. People who jumped into Brisbane in 2018–2020 before it boomed? They're flying.

Meanwhile, people who hesitated are now priced out of those same suburbs and stuck comparing what could've been.

It won't sting you immediately, but it hurts the most long-term.

You don't just lose the money you *could have* made. You lose the options, the flexibility, the freedom.

That's what wealth really gives you, freedom to choose: Work or don't work, live where you want, send your kids to whatever school you want, skip lines at airports & eat nutritious meals on the way to your holiday destination.

Every year you delay wealth creation is another year you handcuff your future self.

You don't have to know everything. You don't have to be fearless. You don't even need to get it 100% right. You just need to do something.

Even if your first property is small, regional, or imperfect, at least you're *in the game*. Because the longer you sit on the bench, the more expensive the price of entry gets.

And that's the thing no one talks about, that doing nothing will cost you more than doing something ever will.

Part 2: Your First Step Into Property

Understanding the Market: *How Property Really Works*

If you want to build wealth through property, the first thing you need to understand is the market isn't magic, it's maths. It's patterns, people, policy, and timing. And once you get your head around that, you'll realise this whole game is actually a lot more predictable than most people think.

I'm going to start with some nerdy stuff and then give you a real cheat code lesson.

The Technical Bits (That Actually Matter)

There are three key drivers of **capital growth**:

1. *Supply & Demand*

When more people want to live somewhere than there are houses available, prices rise. Simple. Like nightclub economics, too many people trying to get into one door, the bouncer raises the price of entry.

2. Population Growth

The more people moving to an area (whether from overseas, interstate, or outer suburbs), the more pressure there is on housing. *So if you're struggling to buy a house, maybe stop voting for the parties that bring in unsustainable levels of immigration haha.* This is why areas with new hospitals, universities, transport links and job hubs pop off before anyone else notices.

3. Infrastructure Investment

When the government drops billions into roads, rail, schools, airports or precincts, follow the money.

Infrastructure = accessibility = desirability = demand = price rise.

Then you've got the micro data points:

- **Vacancy rates** (lower = tighter rental market = good for investors)
- **Median prices** (a good baseline, but don't obsess)
- **Auction clearance rates** (hot = rising prices)
- **Days on market** (shorter = higher demand)
- **Owner-occupier ratios** (a goldmine for long-term capital growth)
- **Gentrification signs** (new cafes, Bunnings, childcare centres = hint of boom)

And the big macro ones:

- **Interest rates** (obviously affect borrowing power)
- **Government policy** (grants, tax policy, first home incentives)
- **Credit policy** (are the banks lending or tightening?)

Smart investors know how to interpret these signals. They don't buy based on "gut feel" or "my uncle at the family BBQ said it's a good opportunity." They look at evidence. They look for tension in the market. They find areas with all the growth signs, and they strike *before* the headlines hit.

Sounds Complicated? It Doesn't Have to Be

Now, you can go full spreadsheet mode and become a property data ninja. That's totally an option. But for 90% of people reading this, you don't need to become an expert in all this. If you want to become a property tycoon, you don't need a degree in economics, you need to get off your arse, make as much money as you can, stop wasting it on crap, and make smart, repeatable decisions.

You don't need a fancy car, you need a deposit. You don't need a new outfit every weekend and to drink at fancy bars, you need borrowing capacity. You don't need to scroll realestate.com.au aimlessly, you need a Buyers Agent who actually does this professionally.

People overcomplicate this stuff. They think buying property is about winning some secret insider game. It's not. It's about discipline, consistency, and not being a muppet with your money.

The Property Game Is Just a System

Here's the cheat code no one teaches you in school:

Property is just a system.

- Earn income
- Save a deposit
- Buy the right asset you can afford
- Let time and compounding do the work
- Refinance, repeat, grow

Eventually, **options appear that most people never get.**

It's never a *get-rich-quick* scheme. They don't exist. Anyone who says they exist, run! But it is a **get — wealthy — in — the — long run — if — you — don't — stuff — it — up — by — making — sh*tty — financial — decisions** scheme.

You can either:

Spend the next decade upgrading your iPhone every year and wondering why you're still renting,

or

Get intentional, buy a property, and be shocked at how quickly things snowball when you get it right.

Saving, Sacrifice & Strategy

The "Out of Sight, Out of Mind" Way to Build Wealth

Let's get something straight, no one ever built a property portfolio or a retirement nest egg because they downloaded an app and "rounded up their spending." You need strategy, you need structure, and yep, you need a little sacrifice.

After I bought my first property, there were plenty of times where I basically lived on Mi-Goreng Noodles & cheap alcohol until I get paid.

But the good news? You don't have to become a monk or live off instant noodles forever. You just need a system that works for your lifestyle and keeps you consistent long enough to get the results.

So let me share with you the system Sarah and I used that completely changed how we handled our money, and ultimately helped us build real wealth.

...I wish I knew it when I was 18.

Most People Budget Backwards

Most people try to save whatever's left over at the end of the month. Let me ask you, how's that working out? Exactly.

Instead, you need to reverse engineer your finances. Every dollar should have a job, and that job should align with your goals, not your impulses.

That's where this system comes in.

The Future Flow™ Banking System

Here's how it works:

1. Main Income Account (Your Command Centre)

Every dollar you earn; wages, side hustle money, rental income, Centrelink payments, even that sneaky $20 your mate finally paid you back, goes into here.

Here's the key: You must choose a new "$0."

This isn't literally $0. This is your emergency float, your baseline. For some people, that's $10k. For others, it's $20k. Work out how much 3–6 months of essential expenses are for you, that's your new zero. You do not let this account fall below that. Ever.

2. Joint Bills Account (The Boring but Essential Stuff)

All your fixed expenses go here:

- Utility bills
- Internet
- Phone plans
- Netflix, Spotify, Amazon, etc

Total up all your bills for the year, divide by 52, and transfer that amount weekly from your Main Income Account. Set and forget. No "bill shock," no arguing about electricity, no scrambling when the rego's due. The money should be there ready to pay.

You might even save money if you pay your regular bills annually instead of monthly.

3 & 4. Personal Spending Accounts (His & Hers)

You each get your own play money. Equal amounts.

This is for:

- » Coffees
- » Clothes
- » Punting (Shhh)
- » Handbags
- » Bunnings runs
- » Gym memberships
- » Whatever makes you feel like an adult with dignity

But here's the deal: if you blow it, you're done until next week. Don't touch the Main Income Account. Don't raid the bills. If you need more, have a conversation with your partner. This is about respect and discipline.

5. Your "Escape" Fund

This one is gold. Figure out how much you want for holidays each year, $5k, $10k, $20k, and divide it by 52. That's your weekly amount. Set up an automatic transfer to a completely separate bank (trust me on this). Out of sight, out of mind.

When it's time to book that Europe trip or head to Fiji, the money's there. No stress or guilt. No credit cards.

6. Wealth Builder (Your Future Freedom Fund)

This is the account that changes your life.

At the end of each month, look at your Main Income Account. Whatever's sitting above your new $0 baseline, move it straight into this account.

Don't even think about it. Just move it, forget it, and watch it grow.

Again, ideally with another bank so it's not just a click away from your daily tap & go spending. This account becomes your deposit for your next property, or the buffer for your investment strategy, or the loan killer to crush your bad debt. Whatever your financial adviser recommends or you decide makes the most sense.

As human beings we're wired to use the means we have available to us. It's called Parkinson's Law. By segmenting your money into buckets, psychologically, you know what each dollar is for. You'll run out of your weekly spending money and think to yourself *"well, I did have a big weekend"* and instead of dipping into your "Holidays" or "Bills" or "Future Wealth" buckets, because that money is already for something else, you'll wait another week to access more "Personal Spending" money.

It'll take some time to get right, but once it's working, it's like a well-oiled machine, with all your Bills paid, all your holidays booked & wealth position improving.

Why This Works

» It removes emotion and guesswork

» It forces conversations about money without yelling

» It separates your short-term dopamine hits from your long-term dreams

» And most importantly it's sustainable.

This is how normal people with normal jobs and normal incomes build extraordinary futures. I built my first $million net wealth as a PAYG Employee. The system isn't stopping you from doing it too.

You don't need a $400k salary. You just need structure, automation, and the guts to say no to shiny crap you don't need... until you can afford it three times over.

How to Buy Your First Property Without Being Rich

Let's cut the fluff. Buying your first property has nothing to do with being rich and everything to do with being focused. Most people don't have a property problem. They have a reality problem.

They spend all their time scrolling listings in Bondi or Brighton, looking at $1.8 million homes with water views... while they earn $70k a year and are spending half of it on Deliveroo and Afterpay.

Let me ask you something: Did your parents buy their dream home, in their dream suburb, in one of the top 3 cities in the world?

No.

They bought what they could afford. In a city that was still developing. They didn't *start* with the dream, they grew into it.

Start Where You Can Buy

If you're trying to buy your dream home first, you've already lost the plot.

What you need to be asking is:

» Where *can* I afford?

» Where is population growth heading?

» Where is new infrastructure being planned?

» Where is the next boom likely to happen?

The answers to those questions will *not* be Surry Hills, South Yarra, or the Gold Coast beachfront.

They'll be places like:

» **Perth outer suburbs** (growth corridor + affordability)
» **South-East Queensland** (more people = more pressure)
» **Regional centres near capital cities** (great value, rising demand)
» **Adelaide's fringes or Perth's north** (with tight vacancy rates and low median prices)

Key tip: follow the **infrastructure pipeline**, not the brunch spots with ladies saying, *"Oh Genevieve, that is a simply divine cashmere twinset. Did you get it from David Jones or that little boutique in Double Bay?"*

Step 1: Talk to a Mortgage Broker (Not Your Mates)

Your first move isn't *realestate.com.au*, it's a meeting with a Mortgage Broker.

Tell them:

> "I want to know what income and savings I need to buy a property worth $400,000 to $500,000."

Ask them:

» What deposit would I need?
» What would repayments look like?
» What are my options with 5% (If you can live in it) or 10% (Investment Property) deposit loans?

- What Government incentives can I use?
- What does my credit look like?

They'll give you a **reality check**, and that's the best gift you'll get on this journey.

Step 2: Go Through Your Expenses with a Fine-Tooth Comb.

Now that you know your target, let's talk about how to hit it. Take your last 3 months of transactions and go through them line by line.
Split them into two lists:

"Needs" = Non-Negotiables

- Groceries
- Rent (basic)
- Transport to work
- Utilities
- Kids' essentials (if you've got them)

"Wants" = Optional Lifestyle Stuff

- Uber Eats
- Netflix
- Weekend benders
- New clothes "just because"
- Takeaway coffees every day
- Subscriptions you forgot you had
- Upgraded phone plans
- That thing you bought because TikTok told you it would change your life

Now be honest with yourself. Are those "wants" really worth staying broke for?

*The Government Pension Should Scare the Sh*t Out of You*

If you're relying on the Government to bail you out in retirement, let me tell you something: You're going to spend your later years hoping that the next election doesn't ruin your life.

You'll be sitting there in your 70s, praying interest rates stay low and power prices stay capped just so you can afford to eat and heat the house.

No thanks.

You do *not* want to be dependent on handouts when you're old. Wanting Government handouts is the biggest scam being pushed in the 21st century in the West.

You want to be:

- Self-sufficient
- Independent
- In control
- Able to help your kids
- And completely unbothered by politicians

And when you are, you'll look back on your younger self who just wanted free sh*t from the Government and just shake your head.

Step 3: Work Out How You'll Get the Deposit

You now know what the bank needs. You know what you're wasting money on. Now comes the big one: how are you going to get that deposit?

Think of every way possible:

- Gift from parents or family
- Selling stuff you don't need (maybe go all in on flip-life). There was a guy that turned a paper clip into a house. What can you do?
- Side hustle or weekend work (make Fairy Floss or baked goods if you have to). Morgan Hipworth made a pop-up store when he was 17 years old and sold $55,000 worth of donuts in his opening 8 days. Then by 19 he was worth $200 million. Legend!
- Asking for a raise (do not be afraid of asking/*demanding* a pay rise). Two things will happen, they'll desperately want to keep you so they'll give you the pay increase, or they'll happily let you go and that's good feedback about yourself. Work harder!
- Changing jobs (I took sideways jobs at different companies all the time, f**k company loyalty, I'm loyal to myself, my family and my own goals, thank you)
- Cutting expenses ruthlessly (Drinking fancy wine isn't worth being poor)
- Refund schemes (450,000 bottles = $45,000, go nuts)
- Launching a once-off idea or event (What's your Waynestock going to be called)
- Or... pulling a "you" move like I did and going all in on a creative once off crazy idea. Just go for it and make it happen.

You only need one strategy to work. The money is out there. You've just got to go get it.

If this is a real goal for you, then go make it real. Stop complaining about results you didn't get from work you didn't do. This isn't a game for victims, it's for people who take responsibility.

No more excuses. No more scrolling dream homes with a beer in one hand and credit card debt in the other.

Put your head down, cut the crap, get the advice, and do whatever it takes to buy that first property. Because once you've got the first one, the next step becomes 10x easier.

And when you're 65 and *not* living on the pension, watching your property portfolio spin off passive income while you play golf or travel with the grandkids. You'll thank yourself a million times over.

Making Money on the Way In: The Power of Research & Buying Well

Most people think you make money in property when it goes up in value. But here's a little secret: The smart ones make money the day they buy. Not from timing the market, not from a crystal ball, but by buying well. And buying well starts with research.

The Good News? Research Is (Mostly) Free (if you have the time)

You don't need a university degree or a million-dollar portfolio to access real property data. If you're willing to put in the time, there are tools available right now, and most of them are completely free.

Here's where to start:

Websites You Can Use

- **Domain & realestate.com.au** – Understand median prices, days on market, and what's trending.
- **SQM Research** – Vacancy rates, rental yields, distressed sales, and market sentiment.
- **CoreLogic suburb reports** – Limited free info but gold if you get your hands on a paid report.
- **Local Council websites** – Zoning plans, infrastructure projects, upcoming developments.
- **Infrastructure Australia project pipeline** – See where the billions are being spent.
- **Microburbs.com.au** – Suburb-level demographic and lifestyle data.
- **Facebook groups** – Watch local buyers and investors talk about their wins and losses in real time.

Spend a couple of weekends geeking out on this stuff and you'll already be ahead of 90% of buyers.

If you decide to use Buyers Agents, they spend enormous amounts of money to gain access to the top economist data available and it's all done for you. But if you want to spend the time on it yourself and learn, there's a few tips to get you started.

Or... Leverage the People Who Do It All Day

Now if you're not the "research-for-fun-on-a-Friday-night" type, there's another way: **Use a Buyers Agent.**

If you can afford one, especially for your first investment, do it. They live and breathe this stuff. They know:

- Where the next gentrification is happening
- Which streets are flood-prone
- What new school zones are about to drive demand
- How to negotiate under market
- Where owner-occupiers are fighting over stock (which drives long-term prices up)

And here's the cool part: Some Buyers Agents offer just the research, for a much lower fee. They'll tell you what to buy, where, and why, you go and secure the deal yourself. If you're time-rich but cash-conscious, that's a perfect combo.

Cosmetic Fixers = Instant Equity

One of the best ways to "buy well" is to look for homes that scare off other buyers.

I'm talking:

- Outdated carpets
- Peach-coloured bathrooms
- Old yellow light fittings
- Granny curtains
- Flaky paint

These properties are goldmines, especially in high owner-occupier areas. Why? Because most people who show up to the open homes don't want to renovate, they're looking for 'done for you'.

But if you:

- » Can recognise solid bones
- » Have a bit of vision
- » And can spend $10–20k on cosmetic upgrades...
- » You could create instant equity.

Get advice from your Accountant, often these improvements (especially on rentals) can come with tax benefits.

You've now added:

- » Equity
- » Tax advantages
- » Better rental appeal
- » Higher yield potential

All from buying the ugliest home on a great street.

Advice Can 10x Your Outcome

You might think, "I'm saving money by doing it myself." But let's look at the reality:

- » You buy a $400k property in an oversupplied unit market... in 7 years it's worth $500k.
- » Your mate uses a Buyers Agent and buys a $500k townhouse in a tightly held, height-restricted suburb... in 7 years it's worth $1.1 million.

That's not just a $100k difference. *That's the difference between one property and financial freedom.*

That's the difference between buying a second property or watching from the sidelines. That's the result of one informed decision.

You don't need 100 good property decisions in your life, you need three or four really smart ones.

Don't just focus on capital growth. Focus on how you buy. Buy with an edge. Use data. Use experience. Use leverage. And if it's not your genius zone, pay someone who lives in it.

Because every time you buy well, you start miles ahead of the pack. That's how you build momentum. That's how you build equity. That's how you build wealth.

Remember, property isn't just about what happens *after* you buy. The smartest investors also make money on the way in.

Part 3: Scaling Your Portfolio

Property #2 and Beyond: *Using Equity and Momentum*

Buying your first property is a massive achievement. Congratulations! Most people never get there. But let me tell you something: the first property is the hardest, after that, momentum starts to build.

Once you're in the market, you're not just saving money anymore, you're building equity.

And that equity? That's your weapon to buy again, and again, and again.

Equity: Your Secret Growth Engine

Let's say you buy your first property for $450,000. You sit on it for 2–3 years, the market moves, you do some minor improvements, and suddenly it's worth $600,000.

That's $150,000 in potential equity.

You didn't work overtime to earn it. You didn't win the lottery. You just bought in the right area, at the right time, and let the market do its thing.

And this is where most people make the mistake: They celebrate the initial gain, maybe post on Facebook about it or even worse, cash in to buy a new Tesla... I've seen that happen way too many times. Funnily enough, I've never seen someone still love their decision in 5 years time. Hmmm.

The smart move would be leverage that equity into another property. Start building that portfolio. Start generating passive income.

Step 1: Know Your Numbers

The first thing to do once you own property: get regular updates on its value.

Sign up for:

- CoreLogic or realestate.com.au property reports
- Suburb sales alerts
- RP Data suburb trackers (some are free through your broker or lender)
- Bank valuation tools (often available in your online banking app)

Then every 6–12 months, have a quick meeting with your Mortgage Broker.

Ask:

- What's my current equity position?
- Based on my income, what would I qualify to buy today?
- What rent could I expect from a second property, and how would that affect my borrowing power?

Remember, it's not just about equity. The bank needs to see you can afford the loan too.

Step 2: Create Equity On Purpose

Don't just wait for the market to grow, give it a nudge.

Here are some quick ways to create equity in your current property:

- » Paint the walls
- » Replace outdated carpets or flooring
- » Add a new vanity or mirror to the bathroom
- » Upgrade lighting
- » Improve outdoor areas with low-cost landscaping
- » Add air-conditioning or ceiling fans
- » Check zoning changes or development plans in your area

Before doing any major works, talk to your Accountant. Some improvements may be tax-deductible, especially on an investment property, and others can help boost your rent or future sale price. If it's not going to help you achieve the next goal, ask yourself whether it's actually worth doing or not.

This is about playing the long game and boosting your leverage for the next step.

Step 3: Keep Your Broker on Speed Dial

Too many people wait until they *want* to buy again before talking to their broker. Big mistake.

You need to be proactive. Because here's what can happen:

- Broker: "Congrats, you've got enough equity to buy another property!"
- You: "Awesome, let's do it."
- Broker: "Bad news, your income isn't high enough to qualify for the next loan."

Game over (property wise). If this happens, speak with your Financial Adviser about other ways you can invest 'now'.

So always ask your broker:

- "What equity do I have access to now?"
- "What income would I need to buy another $400k–$500k property?"
- "What rental income would a new property need to support that purchase?"
- "If I got a raise, how much more could I borrow?"
- "If I paid off this loan or debt, would that help?"

This is how serious investors think. They plan two steps ahead, not just the next one.

Rinse and Repeat

Once you've bought your second property, the formula is the same:

- » Let the market do its thing
- » Add value where you can
- » Track your equity
- » Keep income strong
- » Stay tight with your team (broker + accountant + adviser)
- » When the numbers line up, go again

This is the momentum loop that builds serious portfolios. Not quickly. Not recklessly. But strategically.

Over time, your portfolio snowballs, and your wealth does too.

I wish there was some *secret* I could tell you that only the evil "rich" know about, but it's pretty much as simple as this:

- » **Know your numbers**
- » **Work your butt off** to get the first property
- » **Build the right team**
- » **Know your numbers** (again)
- » **Avoid making stupid mistakes** that we naturally want to do as humans, and
- » **Rinse & repeat that** until you're richer than anyone in your family.

Building the Right Team
(Broker, Buyers Agent, Accountant)

Your Broker, Buyers Agent & Accountant: The Three Pillars of a Winning Strategy

Building a serious property portfolio alone isn't a solo sport. You need a team. A proper, professional, *sharp as hell* team. Because as you move forward, the questions get harder, the stakes get higher, and the wins (or mistakes) start stacking fast. Get the right people in your corner early, and you can compound your results for life.

The Mortgage Broker: *Your Finance Architect & Strategist*

In 2025 and beyond, if you're still walking into a bank branch to ask for a loan, you are absolutely crazy. You are dumb 18-year-old Michael. Stop it! That's like buying a car and only asking one dealership what the price is.

A good Mortgage Broker should:

- » Have access to **60+ lenders**
- » Know **credit policy inside and out**
- » Have a **>95% approval rate**
- » Have a **team of specialists** (assessment, lodgement, settlements, post-settlement service)
- » Be able to **get strategic** with structuring your loans, not just lodge an app and cross their fingers
- » Know exactly what the bank wants to see, and finally...

- Know exactly what you should **NOT** provide the bank because *once they see it, they can't unsee it.*

You could go through 10 Brokers in your investing journey. But eventually, you'll find one or two absolute weapons, and when you do, you hold onto them like gold.

The only time I end up leaving a weapon Mortgage Broker is if he/she has scaled themselves out of their business and I'm no longer actually working with that Broker anymore.

The difference between "approved" and "declined" can come down to one sentence in a credit file, and a great Broker knows exactly what sentence to write.

And the best part? Unless something changes, you don't even pay for their service. Brokers are typically paid by the bank after settlement. Zero cost to you. But, I'd encourage you to respect that.

The Clawback Trap

If you refinance, sell, or pay off your loan within 2 years, your Broker cops a clawback. That means the lender takes their commission back.

Imagine finishing a 3-month project at your job, and your boss saying: *"We've decided to cancel the direction we went with, so we're taking all your pay back."*

That's Broker life.

So if your Broker went above and beyond and you need to refinance or sell early, at least consider their income is being clawed back. Loyalty matters in this game. Brokers understand that life happens. But maybe at least go to them next time, refer them to a friend/family member or if you can't do that, give them a 5-star review on Google.

The Buyers Agent: *Your Market Advantage*

If you're buying your first investment property, use a Buyers Agent to gain data-driven insights.

Unless you want to spend hundreds of hours doing research, flying to nationwide cities, talking to councils, trawling listings, running numbers, doing flood/fire checks and negotiating under market, outsource it.

As they say, *"Blind hustle gets you moving; but a 'smart' strategy gets you somewhere."* The properties I've bought through Buyers Agents were by far the least effort, and delivered the fastest and most rewarding results.

A great Buyers Agent will:

- » Use **data-driven suburb selection**
- » Understand **gentrification cycles**
- » Know where **infrastructure is going in**
- » Study **local zoning restrictions** and **housing supply**
- » Show you **case studies of past clients** who followed similar advice and won big

I've personally worked with three Buyers Agents, some were good enough, one was great, and now, I trust my own research and strategy because I've been through it all.

But if you're early on, this is not the place to cut corners. At the very least, pay for a research-only service from a Buyers Agent (some offer this). You find and negotiate the deal, they help you shortlist and assess it.

That alone can make the difference between a property that goes from $400k → $500k in 7 years vs. one that goes from $500k → $1.1 million in the same timeframe.

It's not about luck. It's about making 3–4 smart decisions early on.

The Accountant: *Your Tax & Structure Strategist*

I'm going to say something that will make some Accountants hate me: a lot of Accountants are sh*t. I've seen way too many people being held back by their Accountants so called *financial advice.*

The trouble with a lot of Accountants is that they don't truly understand making decisions from a wealth creation perspective. It's usually a tax cutting exercise.

Now, no-one wants to give the ATO bonus' but if cutting tax means spending more to lower your taxable income, then that's also going to impact your ability to buy property or invest elsewhere.

In the long run, the people accepting the tax & using their profit to buy appreciating assets, win in the end.

Here's some ways you can know if your Accountant is one of them...

If:

- You get an email every 3 months with your BAS
- Once a year, they send you a tax return
- You don't hear from them unless *you* reach out
- ...and they never really ask you questions or provide you 'advice'.

You don't have an Accountant, you've got a compliance checker. They're called an Accountant, but they're not advising you, they're keeping you out of trouble. That's all.

A proper Accountant, in my eyes, one worth keeping, will:

- Meet with you at least once a year (ideally more) and ask about your next 12 month plans, not just your past 12
- Help you plan 3–5 years ahead for tax, structure and business moves

» Be across changes in legislation before you hear about them (if you are seriously impacted by a new legislation change and you don't hear about it for 12 months, I would be seriously considering changing Accountants unless they have a damn good reason).
» Help you think *strategically*, not just check and tick compliance boxes.

And if you're building a property portfolio? You want one who understands investment structures like:

» Company vs trust vs personal
» Land tax thresholds
» Passive income strategies
» Estate planning
» CGT impacts and future-proofing

If you become wealthy in your personal name, your tax bill will haunt you for the rest of your life and when you die, your kids will cop an even bigger hit.

The ATO will throw the biggest Christmas party ever the year you pass.

All those assets shifting hands? Huge tax event. And all avoidable, *if* you got good advice early.

Now yes, Accountants can't give you financial advice on shares, super etc, you'll need a Financial Adviser for that.

But if your main game is property? A smart Accountant who understands portfolio structure and taxation advice will save you hundreds of thousands in tax over your lifetime.

Your **Broker** helps you borrow smarter and avoid dead ends.

Your **Buyers Agent** helps you buy better and grow faster.

Your **Accountant** helps you keep more of what you build.

This is your core three. If you want to be a serious investor, treat this like assembling your Grand Final team. No passengers. No "my cousin's mate does tax on the side." No fluff. Find the A-players, and you'll thank yourself every year from now on.

Because property isn't just about bricks and mortar, it's about people and strategy.

And with the right team behind you? You're unstoppable.

Avoiding Rookie Mistakes

Most people don't fail in property because they're lazy. They fail because they *don't know what they don't know*. And when you're starting out, big mistake can be costly and set you back years.

One wrong suburb, one bad structure, one emotional purchase... and you can stall your momentum for years and these types of mistakes can cost you a lot.

So in this chapter, I'm going to call out the biggest rookie mistakes I've seen (and in some cases, made myself), so you can sidestep them completely.

Mistake #1: Stop Flaunting Wealth You Do NOT Have.

The Fastest Way to Stay Broke Forever

Let me be brutally honest with you: Most people are faking it. The car, the watch, the holidays, the "top shelf" weekends away, none of it's real. It's just a loud mask covering a financially fragile life.

As soon as their 'active' income goes away, boom. Reality!

You would be shocked at how many 63 year olds have the pre-golden years realisation that their life is about to drastically change when they retire. Don't be that person!

These people who are in their 30's & 40's and out there drinking fancy bottles of wine they can't pronounce, test-driving a Porsche, and planning a $4,000 long weekend like they're Andrew Tate's cousin will most likely have a rude shock later in life.

And look, I'm all for enjoying your life. But not when you're doing it with money you actively worked for and haven't invested a cent into your future.

Because here's what I promise you...

If you're blowing every pay rise on lifestyle inflation instead of building assets, don't play the victim when the government raises the pension age to 80 and your knees can't even walk up the stairs.

You are your own problem.

The Myth of "I Deserve It"

We've all heard it; "I've worked so hard... I deserve to upgrade my car.," "I've earned this weekend away." or "I'm finally earning six figures, I should be living a little."

Look, you do deserve to enjoy life. But you also deserve not to be stressed about money for the next 40 years.

If your income increases and your spending matches it, you're not richer. You're just better at pretending. There's no award for "Best Financial Illusion."

Hedonic Adaptation

There's a well-documented concept in behavioural economics that describes this, it's called "hedonic adaptation," the tendency for people to quickly return to a baseline level of satisfaction, no matter what positive (or negative) changes happen in their life.

So you might imagine the Lambo, the Rolex, the business class flights... and it gives you a little mental holiday. A high. But once you've actually done the work and have the money to afford it, I promise you, you realise you don't even want it anymore.

Because the buzz was never in owning the *thing*, it was in escaping your current life. People with no money fantasise about Lambos. People with real wealth are more interested in buying back their time.

So whenever I hear people wearing fancy clothes and saying *"Yeah, my plan is to buy a Lambo in a few years,"* I just smile and think, *"you'll grow up eventually, kid."*

Wealthy people would rather take their kids to school every morning, or wake up without an alarm, or spend Thursday on the golf course, than park an Italian engine in the driveway they never have time to drive.

I was lucky enough to have people talk some sense into me about money from a younger age. My perspective about unnecessary cars hasn't changed for as long as I can remember "I'm not buying a nice car until I can park it in a lock-up garage, in a good suburb, at a house that I own and I can fund the car with passive income."

A new bodykit for a Lambo is like $60,000 and you're going to pay for that with your *active* income? Stupid!

There's a lot to unpack there. For me, property is more important than cars. Setting my family up with a nice home, in a good area, with safety and security absolutely comes before *"nice car, bro."* I need to pay off my PPR mortgage. I need to have enough assets that generate enough passive income to fund my life, family, schools, lifestyle before I even think about a fancy car.

Don't get me wrong, if you check my browser history, you'll still find me deep in a Carsales scroll looking at dream cars I'll probably buy one day. But for now? I drive a 2019 Toyota Corolla I bought brand new. Toyota calls frequently telling me I'm pre-approved for some big number and I could drive away in one of their top-end 79 series models tomorrow. But honestly... I don't need it, and who am I trying to impress? We've got a Prado for off-road trips. The Corolla starts every time, gets me from A to B without a hiccup, and costs next to nothing to run. That's all I need right now.

And if you read that and think *"I'm not going to listen to him, I drive a better car than he does"* then you have completely missed the point of building wealth. You might need to read the mindset chapter again.

There's nothing wrong with dreams & goals. You just need to be smarter with the order in which you achieve those dreams & goals. Don't get your priorities mixed up!

Mistake #2: Shopping for Your Dream Home Instead of a Smart Investment

Your first property is not your forever home. It's your launchpad.

Don't get caught emotionally chasing suburbs with rooftop brunch cafés, $20 smoothies, and white Range Rovers. If you're trying to build wealth, follow the infrastructure, not the sourdough.

Your parents didn't start in a global city with sky-high prices. They bought what they could afford, where growth was happening. So you need to flip your mindset from **"Where do I want to live?"** to **"Where are the jobs, people and money heading?"**

Mistake #3: Not Knowing Your Numbers

Too many rookies fall in love with a property without knowing:

- What equity they've got
- What income they need for the next purchase
- What the repayments will be at different interest rates
- What the bank will actually lend them

Speak to your Mortgage Broker early. And I don't mean once. I mean regularly.

Ask:

- "What would I need to buy again?"
- "How does rental income factor in?"
- "If I get a raise, clear a debt or cancel this Buy-Now-Pay-Later service, how does that help?"

Equity comes fast. Income capacity doesn't. So plan ahead, or you'll get stuck with growth you can't leverage.

Mistake #4: Trying to Do It All Yourself

You wouldn't build a house without tradies. So don't try to build a portfolio without experts.

Find a killer:

- **Mortgage Broker**, not just any Broker. One with >95% approval rates, a proper team supporting them, and experience with real investment lending.
- **Buyers Agent**, even if you just use their research-only service. Data-driven, no hype & case studies of success.
- **Accountant**, one who actually talks to you and plans 3–5 years ahead. Not a tax-time compliance checker emailer.

Trying to save $3,000 now could cost you **$300,000 in missed gains** later. Or worse, could cost you or your kids $300,000 (or more) in taxes later.

Mistake #5: High-Rise Apartments in Oversupplied Areas

On paper, it looks good. "Modern! Affordable! In the city!"

But dig deeper:

- High density = more supply = slower growth
- Massive strata fees chew up your yield
- Resale can be a nightmare
- Developers usually win. You usually don't.

Instead, look at areas with:

- Height restrictions
- >70% Owner-occupier
- Limited new supply
- Desirable school zones, transport upgrades or other infrastructure and labour markets.

A $500k townhouse in the next suburb with all those fundamentals will outperform the $350k high rise apartment 10 times over.

Mistake #6: Ignoring Cosmetic Renovation Opportunities

Want instant equity? *Consider* buying something that's solid but ugly.
If a property ticks all the boxes but it just needs:

- Paint
- Carpet or flooring
- A new vanity
- Light fittings
- Some curb appeal...

...and it's in a strong owner-occupier area, you might just be able to buy it under market because no one else wants to do the work.

Fix it before the tenant moves in, **talk to your Accountant** about the tax benefits, and boom, you've just boosted your equity, yield, and long-term position.

Mistake #7: Trusting the Wrong Accountant

Most Accountants are compliance checkers. You need one who's a strategist.

If your Accountant:

- » Only emails you tax returns once a year
- » Never talks about next year or the next five
- » Isn't helping you understand structures (trusts, companies, etc)
- » Has never asked about your long-term financial goals

You've got the wrong one. And if you build a big portfolio in your own name without advice, you could get hammered by tax now, later, and when you die.

Don't let the ATO throw a Christmas party in your honour.

Mistake #8: Underestimating the Power of Momentum

As the saying goes, *"people overestimate what they can achieve in 12 months and massively underestimate what can happen in 10 years."* Something like that.

The second you buy your first property, start planning for your second.

Track the value with datafeeds and speak with your Broker. Watch your equity build. While you work on your next income target. Get rental estimates for your next potential purchase.

Because most people wait until their Broker says "You've got the equity!" only to hear "But sorry... you don't have the income."

Don't let that be you. You don't have to be perfect. You just have to avoid being dumb.

You don't need to know everything. You just need to learn from those who've gone before you.

If you avoid the rookie mistakes, you'll get there faster, you'll build smarter, you'll keep more of what you make and you'll actually enjoy the process instead of stressing over every decision

Your future self will thank you. And your past self, the one reading this right now, will know they did the right thing.

Part 4: Structure, Strategy & Smart Decisions

Ownership Structures: *Trusts, Companies, SMSFs Explained Simply*

When most people buy their first property, they don't think too much about ownership structure. It's definitely a lot easier to just "Whack it in my name, sign the paperwork, job done." Right? I did.

And to be fair, that's probably fine for a lot of people starting out. Especially if you're going to live in it. But if you plan to build a serious investment portfolio? You want to at least understand the options. Because how you own your properties can have a massive impact on your tax, your control, your future estate planning, and your ability to keep more of what you build.

This chapter is NOT about telling you what to do, because the right structure for **you** depends on **your** situation. So I'll say this loud and clear:

This is NOT financial advice. Always speak with your Accountant before making any structural decisions.

Let's break the options down in plain English.

1. Personal Name

This is the most common way people buy property, in their own name or jointly with a partner.

Pros:

- Super simple to set up
- Cheapest to run (no annual company/trust fees)
- Easy finance, banks love it
- Capital gains tax discounts apply for individuals

Cons:

- **You personally wear all the liability** (if something goes wrong, someone wants to take you to court, it comes back to *you*)
- If you become wealthy in your personal name, you could be paying **very high tax rates** for life
- On death, passing these assets to kids/beneficiaries can result in **huge tax events**
- Your income from rent or sales gets taxed at your personal tax rate

So, it works fine for one or two properties, especially early on, but it can get expensive, really quickly, if you don't plan ahead.

2. Trusts (Family Trusts or Discretionary Trusts)

A Trust isn't a person or a company, it's a structure that holds assets on behalf of others. Think of it like a legal "bucket" that you control, but you're not taxed personally on what it earns.

Pros:

- Flexibility to **distribute income** to different beneficiaries (e.g. your spouse, adult children)
- Can help manage and **minimise tax** if used properly
- Offers a degree of **asset protection** from lawsuits or business risks
- Useful for **generational wealth transfer** (avoids direct ownership complications)

Cons:

- Costs more to set up and maintain
- Can't access capital gains tax discounts if the property is sold through a company inside a trust
- Can be harder to finance if you're new or don't have strong income
- You'll need to file separate tax returns for the trust and keep good records
- Great structure for protecting wealth and distributing income, but definitely not something to set up without proper advice.

3. Companies

This is when you buy property in a company's name, usually a proprietary limited company (Pty Ltd).

Pros:

- Flat corporate tax rate (usually lower than top personal rates)
- Clear separation of personal and business assets
- More attractive for commercial property and developments
- Liability is limited to the company, not you personally

Cons:

- No capital gains discount, companies pay full CGT
- Not ideal for long-term hold residential property (unless part of a strategy)
- More complex accounting, ongoing ASIC fees
- Harder to pull money out without extra tax
- Generally better for business income or short-term projects than long-term residential investing, but it depends.

4. SMSF (Self-Managed Super Fund)

This is when you can use your super to invest in property, usually through a Self-Managed Super Fund.

Now, apologies if this gets a bit ranty, but it needs to be said. SMSF's are probably the most backwards part of the financial services industry. You need an Accountant to set it up. But an Accountant cannot advise you on whether you *should* have an SMSF or not.

Just think about that for a second. They can set it up for you, but they cannot advise you whether you should have it. Why? Because Accountants cannot give you financial advice. SMSF is a financial product. To me that is absolutely wild.

You need to speak with a Financial Adviser to decide whether or not you *should* have one and when I worked closely with financial advisers for many years it was a consensus that probably 90% of the people in Australia that have a SMSF, shouldn't have one.

Normally the reason they have one is because they were talked into it by this "property expert" and this "Accountant." Usually they work together to sell you properties you shouldn't buy because they make a lot of money.

What happens is people start selling properties, more than likely *off-the-plan,* and tell you if you have more than $80,000-$100,000 in your Super you can buy one. We've all seen those *dirty* ads. They're very careful about not saying they advised you to do it. So without advising you whether a SMSF makes sense for your financial situation, you're just agreeing to do it anyway, the Accountant sets it up for you, then they sell your SMSF a property and make a *lot of money* out of you. Typically those people selling properties off the plan can be making up to 12% of the purchase price as their commission. *And,* you're paying for it.

Just think about that next time you hear "oh you can claim the depreciation," what is depreciation? It's when you bought your asset for more than it's actually worth.

The thing with SMSF is there are so many legalities, fees and higher interest rates that if your balance isn't enough a SMSF ends up holding you back, rather than propelling you forward. At one point ASIC recommended $500,000 as a combined Super balance (with your partner) as an indicator of the "appropriateness of advice" before opening a SMSF. That's since been removed, which was welcomed by the SMSF Association. SMSF Association is now leaning more towards $200,000.

https://www.smsfassociation.com/news-articles/why-you-need-more-than-just-200000-to-start-your-own-super-fund

I have my own opinions, but...

My recommendation, absolutely 100%, is to get advice from a Registered Financial Adviser before going ahead with a SMSF. Your Accountant most likely isn't giving you financial advice, unless they're also a Registered Financial Adviser and presenting you with a "Statement of Advice," so just double check.

Now, in saying all of that, I'm in the process of starting one up with my adviser. But I've got the Super balance to support it. We're going to buy our dream retirement home. Rent it out for 25 years and then move into it (if the house isn't falling to pieces). When SMSF makes sense for you, they can be a really great wealth builder. But not before.

Pros:

- Lower tax rates inside super
  (15% income, 0–10% capital gains if conditions met)
- Growth happens inside your retirement fund
- Great way to diversify super away from just shares or managed funds

Cons:

- The property must be for retirement purposes, not personal use
- Very strict rules, the property must be bought with SMSF's money, rented out at market rates, no personal use
- Complex setup and compliance
- Financing is more restrictive and interest rates are higher
- Selling or withdrawing profits is locked up until preservation age

This structure can work really well for long-term tax planning, but it's absolutely not DIY territory. You'll need solid legal and accounting support to do this properly.

So... Why Not Just Use Your Own Name?

Here's the thing, buying property in your own name is fine until it's not.

When:

- Your income starts climbing
- You own multiple properties
- You want to leave wealth to your kids
- Or protect your assets from risk...

...owning everything in your personal name can get expensive and messy, especially when tax bills or estate planning come into play.

And like I said earlier, the day you die and all your properties are in your own name is the day the ATO throws a champagne party. The tax implications of transferring all those assets can be huge.

There is no one-size-fits-all structure. The best structure for YOU depends on:

- » Your current income
- » Your family situation
- » Your future plans
- » Whether you run a business
- » And how many properties you plan to own

So again, speak to your Accountant. A good one will ask the right questions and tailor a structure to suit your goals and protect your wealth.

Don't set up a trust just because you heard it was smart. Don't avoid a company just because it sounds scary. And don't assume your personal name is the best just because it's easy.

Play the long game and structure your ownership like someone who plans to win.

Managing Risk:
Insurance, Buffers, and Contingencies

Because Wealth Is Useless If You Can't Hold Onto It

Here's something most people get wrong about building wealth: It's not just about how much you make, it's about how well you protect it.

Ask any seasoned investor or entrepreneur and they'll tell you that managing risk is half the game.

You can make the right property decisions, stack the right investments, build momentum, but if one thing goes wrong (say health wise or floods/ bushfires) and you're not protected, it can all come crashing down.

This chapter isn't about *doom and gloom*, it's about playing smart and respecting the game. Because once you start building wealth, the goal is no longer just to make money, it's to keep it.

Insurance for me just removes all anxiety of what 'could' go wrong.

Step One: Protect Your Income

Let's start with the obvious.

Most people have:

- Car insurance
- Health insurance
- Phone insurance
- Home & contents insurance

But the one thing that pays for all of those, their *income,* is the one thing they don't insure. Let that sink in.

Your income:

- Pays the mortgage
- Feeds the kids
- Pays the school fees
- Covers your lifestyle
- Funds your investments
- Builds your future

Lose your income and everything else is at risk. That's why it might be worth speaking with a licensed Financial Adviser to explore things like:

- Income Protection Insurance
- Total and Permanent Disability (TPD) Cover
- Life Cover (especially if you've got kids or a mortgage)

And no, this is not financial advice. This is common sense. You'd never drive an uninsured $30k car, but you'll risk your $2 million lifetime income stream? Think about that.

Step Two: Build a Buffer

This one's simple but powerful, have cash set aside. You can call it an emergency fund, a contingency account, a cash buffer, it doesn't matter what name you slap on it.

How much? That's up to you, but a good rule of thumb is 3–6 months of expenses. If you've got a property portfolio, you might want more than that. And just quietly, if you're investing while sitting on zero cash buffer, you're gambling, not investing.

Step Three: Think in Contingencies

This is where most people get lazy, they assume everything will go to plan.

But here's how serious investors think:

» "What if the tenant stops paying rent?"

» "What if interest rates go up?"

» "What if I lose my job?"

» "What if we need to sell quickly, will we be okay?"

That doesn't mean you get scared off. It means you build a plan.

Here's what that can look like:

» Make sure every property can be rented at a fair rate, even in a down market

» Don't stretch yourself to the point where *everything* needs to go right

» Have a second opinion on your numbers; Broker, Accountant, Adviser

» Know your exit strategies; sell, refinance, redraw equity, reduce exposure

It's not about being pessimistic. It's about being prepared.

Don't Be the Hero

When you're early in the game, you're not invincible. You're financially fragile. You haven't built enough yet. You're not diversified yet. So if one major thing goes wrong, it hurts 10x more.

This is why protecting your downside is so important in the beginning. Once you've got a few properties, income streams, maybe a business and some shares, you can absorb shocks. Until then? Play smart.

Cover your income. Build your buffer. Have your exit plan. And know that contingency is not weakness, it's wisdom.

Knowing Your Numbers: *Cash Flow, Capital Growth, Yield*

This isn't the most sexy part of it, but it separates the investors from the dreamers.

You've probably heard this a few times already in this book, but it's worth repeating. If you don't know your numbers, you're not investing, you're guessing.

It doesn't matter how nice the property looks or how many other people are bidding at the open home, if the numbers don't make sense, you're setting yourself up for a future headache.

Let's keep it simple and focus on the big three.

Cash Flow

This is your day-to-day. Think of it like your heart rate while running. If you keep your heart rate at a manageable level, you can run 10x longer than if you sprint straight away and run out of gas. That's cashflow.

It's the energy that's coming in and the energy that's going out. You want to know what rent you're getting, what your repayments are, your property management fees, insurance, council rates, repairs, and everything else.

Once you've got that sorted, work out what's left. Is the property putting money in your pocket each week (Positively Geared), is it neutral, or is it costing you (Negatively Geared)? Some negative cash flow is fine if the growth justifies it, but only if it fits within your overall strategy and you can afford it without losing sleep.

Capital Growth

This is the real wealth creator. What's your property worth now, and what's the long-term upside?

Capital growth doesn't happen randomly; it's driven by population growth, infrastructure upgrades, supply and demand, local job opportunities, and gentrification. That's why we keep saying follow the infrastructure, not the Frank Green water bottles.

If you get this part right, the market will do more for your wealth than your job ever could.

Yield

Yield is just your rent divided by the purchase price, shown as a percentage. It gives you a snapshot of how hard your money is working.

If you're getting $500 a week on a $500,000 property, that's roughly a 5% yield. I usually divide by 50, because depending on the state you're buying, you lose 1-2 weeks rent to find a new tenant, so I like to factor that in when doing my numbers. It's better to have extra money than not enough in your buffers.

A high yield might sound great, but sometimes that just means no one wants to live there long term and growth might be dead. You'll see that a lot in Holiday spots & Mining towns.

A slightly lower yield in a booming market will often beat a high-yield, low-growth dud suburb over the long haul.

Track it All

You don't need some fancy software to track your numbers. Just keep a spreadsheet or use a tool like Property Tracker. Personally, I just use a simple Google Sheet and an app called "MyProsperity," with the important details:

- » Rent
- » Mortgage repayments
- » Property expenses
- » Estimated value
- » Equity
- » Buffer

Check it once a month or quarterly at most. Once you've got a few properties, this stuff becomes essential. You shouldn't spend more than 20-30 minutes a month managing it.

If you want a platform to set it all up, you're welcome to use my FutureFocus™ Property Strategy Platform. There's limited access for free, follow this link:
URL: https://www.gameplans.com.au/users/sign_up?code=avidhawks
Code: avidhawks

Renovation vs. New Builds vs. Off-The-Plan

There's no one-size-fits-all when it comes to the type of property you buy. Renovators, new builds, off-the-plan deals; they all have their place. But they each come with different risks, timelines, trade-offs and outcomes. So you need to know what you're really getting into before jumping in.

Let's break them down.

Renovator Delights

Renovator properties used to be absolute gold for investors. You'd find something rough around the edges, grab it for $200k to $300k under market value, throw $80k to $100k into it, and you'd walk away with a tidy equity uplift and better rent. These days? Not so much.

Shows like *The Block* have made everyone think they're a renovation expert. Now you're lucky if you get a $150k discount on a property that still needs $100k worth of work. You've got tradies booked months out, renovation costs have gone up, and council permits are harder than ever to get through.

And don't forget the time and mental load. Organising quotes, chasing up builders, making sure the job gets done right, it's not *passive* in any way. It's a lot of weekends and late nights if you're managing it yourself.

So yeah, you might still make it work, but by the time you factor in the time, the stress, the costs, and the smaller discount, sometimes it just makes more sense to buy something that's already done and ready to go.

That's your call to make. Just make sure you're buying it for the right reasons, not because you think you'll turn into Scott Cam overnight.

New Builds

New builds definitely have their place. They're fresh, they're low maintenance, and tenants usually love them. You'll get depreciation benefits, your Accountant will smile, and in most cases you'll avoid big maintenance costs early on.

The catch is, you often pay a premium for being the first one in. You're buying the "new car smell," not necessarily the best deal.

And don't fall into the trap of thinking depreciation is the win. Depreciation literally means your asset is losing value. That's not how wealth is built. Tax deductions are handy, but they're not the goal.

New builds can still work well if they're in the right suburb with high demand, not much competition, and good growth potential. But don't buy a shiny house in a crap suburb just because it's new.

Off-The-Plan (Approach With Caution)

I'm not going to lie to you, I've bought an off-the-plan property before. In fact, my third property was off-the-plan and it's actually performed really well.

But I didn't buy it off some bloke in a suit at a display home. I bought it because a Buyers Agent I trusted recommended it, showed me the data behind it, and only worked with high quality, reputable builders.

But for a lot of people, that's not how it plays out.

Here's the reality. A developer often finds a big block of land, sometimes in the middle of nowhere, throws together 300 or 500 townhouses that all look the same, and starts flogging them through huge marketing campaigns.

There's no major drivers for future capital growth in the area.

They pour money into brochures and sales displays, pay reps huge commissions, and sell it at inflated prices that include every single cost they've had; marketing, construction, sales commissions, loan interest. Everything.

Then once they sell the last townhouse, they flick off the lights and move on to the next project. No one talks about the estate anymore, the values drop, and sometimes people struggle to get loans approved because the bank won't value the property anywhere near what they paid for it.

That's a nightmare.

And it happens a lot more than you'd think. People get talked into it by someone *pretending* to be a Buyers Agent, when they're actually just a glorified salesperson getting 20 to 30 percent commission on that stock.

Off-the-plan *can* work, it did for me. But would I do it again? Not entirely sure. And I've seen too many people lose sleep and money over the wrong ones. Just be careful.

What to Look Out For

If you're even considering an off-the-plan or new build, ask yourself:

- » **Who's the builder?** Are they any good? Are they being sued? What's their Google reviews like? Read their 1 Star Reviews. Are they winning reputable Building awards?
- » **Who's selling it to me?** Are they actually working for me or just pushing stock? How do they get paid? Am I paying them or is the Builder. Follow the money and you'll find who they work for.
- » **Can I see proper comparable sales of similar properties in the area?** Do some research on future infrastructure. Don't be bought into what 'they' say the future looks like, do some research.

» **What's around?** Are there schools, transport, jobs, and infrastructure already there or just "in the pipeline"?

If the answers aren't clear or you're being given the runaround once you start asking questions, walk away.

Trust the numbers. Not the marketing.

When to Sell, When to Hold

You'll hear a lot of people in property say things like "never sell" or "hold for life," and yeah, that can work, *if* you've got the cash flow to support it and the properties are performing.

But the truth is, you hold property for as long as it makes sense. If you're holding something that's not going up in value, draining your cash every month, and you've got better places to put your equity, then you need to make the tough call.

And if you're ever in a position where you're choosing between foreclosure or selling, then yeah, you do what you need to do. It's not ideal, but survival is more important than pride. Otherwise, you should be thinking long term, and holding as long as possible.

When Selling Might Make Sense

Here are a few examples of when selling could be a smart move:

» You're negatively geared and the property isn't increasing in value

» You've hit a financial ceiling and want to reposition your capital into something higher performing
» A financial adviser has recommended a restructure to improve income as you move towards retirement
» Your life has changed and the property just doesn't serve its purpose anymore

The key isn't just *selling*. The key is *what you do next*. If you're going to sell, make sure you're reinvesting into something that's got better long-term upside, not just sitting on the cash or blowing it on a lifestyle upgrade, like a car.

My Story

I'll give you a real example. My first property sat around $600k to $650k for over a decade. It had done well early on, but eventually it just stopped growing. I held it for ages, trying to do the right thing, but the writing was on the wall.

Around 2012, they started building a whole bunch of high-rise apartment blocks nearby. One would finish, the next would start. It became this endless cycle of supply. All the new buildings were closer to the train station, they had newer appliances, flashier amenities, and mine just became less desirable.

Every time a new development went up, the value of mine went sideways. And they weren't stopping either, I looked into it and there was still 15 to 20 years of supply locked in.

So, I sold it. Not because I was in trouble or needed the money, but because I had a better play. I used the cash to help fund our acreage dream property. Something that has limited supply, is highly desirable, and has massive long-term capital growth potential. That property is going to explode in value over the years. And more importantly, it serves our life-style too.

What did I learn from that experience?

Buying an apartment in a densely populated city area isn't the smartest investment decision. I know that now and would never recommend a client to buy that property. But, it was my first property, I lived in it, it served a purpose for a while and then it didn't.

The problems with it were:

» A massive oversupply of similar or better properties = Capital Growth Stagnation

» Low Land-to-Asset Ratio.

» High Strata/Body Corporate Fees - Considering it didn't have anything major (Eg. Pools or Gyms), the fees kept increasing each quarter.

» Poor Demographic Appeal.

» Undesirable meant that it occasionally had downward pressure on rental yield.

» Finance & Valuation Issues - The banks were always conservative.

» Poor Resale Demand - We struggled to sell it, but got there in the end.

» Ongoing Maintenance Problems - 60 Years Old so there were large building issues occurring regularly which drowned our Strata Sinking Fund.

Access to transport. 1-2km walk to the Train Station. The beautiful thing about me making these kinds of mistakes and sharing my experience is that I can ensure others do not make the same mistakes.

What You Should Consider Before Selling

Before you even think about listing a property, ask yourself:

- Is this property still helping me achieve my goals?
- Is it positively or negatively geared and is that still sustainable?
- What's happening with supply and demand in the area?
- What would I do with the money if I sold today?
- Have I spoken to a Financial Adviser or Accountant to understand the tax implications?
- Do I have a Buyers Agent ready to help me find the next move?

If the answers line up, and you've got a better plan on the other side, then you'll work out your answer. Hold it if it's helping. Sell it if there's a better path forward. Just make sure the decision is based on data, logic, and advice, not emotion.

Part 5: Building an Empire

Scaling with Purpose: *What's Your End Game?*

A lot of people get caught up in building a portfolio just for the sake of building it. More properties, more loans, more equity. And while that's all great, you've got to stop at some point and ask yourself, what's the actual goal here?

What's the end game?

Do you want to live off passive income? Leave something to the kids? Retire early? Buy your dream home? Work part-time? Travel with your partner?

My goal was to live in our dream home, spend every day with my kids, have a Jet-Ski & a Motorbike, play Golf all the time and go on holidays all the time. We're already there. I've still got a lot of life left and I'll keep building, but at no point will building something outweigh getting my time back.

The goal should be getting your time back as much as possible and then keeping it. So for me, if buying a property meant that I had to go back to work, then I'm not buying it. Until the goal changes, my investment philosophy doesn't change.

If you only want to work with someone who owns 70+ properties, then all good, I'm not for you, because I actually have no interest in being that guy. But if your goal is to spend everyday with your kids and go on holidays all the time, I can help you do that.

Firstly, you need to know the finish line, otherwise you'll keep stacking properties and debt without ever knowing when enough is enough. And worse, you could miss your own version of success while chasing someone else's.

Start With the Number

If your goal is financial freedom or early retirement, there's a very simple framework you can use. It's called the 25x Rule.

The idea is super simple. Work out how much income you'd need each year in retirement, then multiply that number by 25. That's the amount of net wealth (excluding your own home) you'll need to fund that lifestyle without ever running out of money.

Why 25x? Because 1 divided by 25 equals 4%, and 4% is generally seen as a safe withdrawal rate from your investments that allows your money to last indefinitely. That's known as the 4% Rule, backed by the famous Trinity Study, a respected piece of research used by financial planners worldwide.

So for example:

- If you want $100,000 per year in income during retirement
- $100,000 × 25 = $2.5 million net worth needed (across all income-generating assets)

That $100k per year can come from rent, share dividends, Super drawdown, interest in savings, or a mix of everything. The point is, it's sustainable, and you don't need to draw down the capital.

Before acting on anything, I'd always recommend speaking with your Registered Financial Adviser so they can map this out for you based on your own personal needs, goals and expectations. This is just a rough guide you can find anywhere.

It's the one I use.

So... What's Your Number?

Don't just pick a random goal. Sit down and think about what your lifestyle actually looks like.

- Do you want to live in a big city or a coastal town?
- Will your house be paid off?
- How much will you spend on travel, hobbies, eating out, and family?
- Are you funding kids' school or helping them with a deposit?
- Do you want to work part-time or not at all?

Once you know the number, you can reverse engineer a strategy to get there.

How Your Portfolio Plays a Role

Let's say you want that same $100,000 per year in income. How could you realistically get there?

Here's an example mix:

» 3–4 properties, each generating $15,000–$20,000 per year in positive rental income
» $500,000–$700,000 in Super, drawing 4–5% per year
» $300,000 in share investments, paying dividends and capital growth
» $100,000–$200,000 sitting in cash or offset accounts as buffer and flexibility, earning interest.

That's just one simple example, but the point is, you don't need 20 properties. You don't even need 10. You just need the *right* assets, structured properly, with a clear outcome in mind.

Every time you buy a property, make sure it's actually taking you closer to the goal. Ask yourself: Will this help me increase my income later in life? Will this give me options or tie me down? Is this property part of a long-term strategy, or am I just buying it because I can?

Too many investors end up with a bunch of average properties that are hard to manage, don't grow in value, and drain their cash flow, all because they never took the time to define the end game.

I've seen it all the time. People online say "I'm in the top 1% of property investors" then you look at the properties they own and they're doing nothing or "I've got a $35million property portfolio" but they haven't really worked out or at least articulated their end goal. To each to their own, I guess. I'd prefer to know what I'm working towards so I know when I get there.

Property as a Vehicle for Freedom, *Not Just Wealth*

Yes, property can build wealth, it can make you a millionaire on paper, it can generate cash flow, open up borrowing capacity, and create equity you can leverage for more growth. That's all great.

But wealth, in itself, isn't the goal. Money is never the goal. Money is the 'tool' I use to get me to the goal.

Why do you work in a job you hate? Money.

What stops you from quitting? Money.

What stops you from telling your boss to f**k off? You don't want to lose money.

Having money means you have the freedom to quit that job you hate.

Goal: Quit that job you hate.

Tell Boss to f**k off... maybe haha.

Money gets you there.

That's as simple as I can make it.

Freedom is the goal, for me anyway.

Too many people chase property just to say they've got "X" number of properties, or they want a million-dollar net worth, or they want to hit a certain figure on paper. But the real power of property is when you use it to buy back your time, your choices, and your lifestyle.

That's real wealth. Not the cars, not the labels, not the social media flex, freedom.

Build It With Purpose

When you're looking at properties, ask yourself:

- Does this get me closer to the life I want?
- Will this reduce my workload down the track?
- Am I buying this because it makes sense, or because it makes me feel like I'm doing something?

A $400,000 property in the right suburb, with the right fundamentals and the right rental return, can buy you more peace and flexibility than a $1.2 million apartment in a city that's all hype and no substance.

Focus on what the property gives you, not just what it's worth on paper or how cool you'll look on social media.

Leaving a Legacy: *Generational Wealth with Intention*

For the first time in Australian history, we're entering a space where intergenerational wealth is not just a concept for the super-rich, it's something every day Aussies need to start thinking about.

In places like Italy, France, England and across much of Europe, the idea of passing wealth down through generations has been normal for centuries. You don't just buy your first home in Rome or London, you're more likely to inherit something or have your parents help you with the leg up. It's built into the culture. It's how families stay ahead generation after generation.

Now, we're seeing the same thing starting to play out here. It's already happening in Sydney. Young people can't get in, not because they're lazy or spending $12 on smoothies (partly that), but because real estate has outpaced incomes to the point that inheritance is becoming one of the few realistic ways in.

But here's the thing; wealth without wisdom is a waste.

Earn It, Spend It, Lose It

There's a well-known cycle; First generation earns it. Second generation spends it. Third generation starts all over again.

And it's true. You see it all the time. Someone busts their arse building a portfolio, running a business, setting up a solid financial foundation... only for the next generation to blow it on stupid decisions, because they never had to earn it and were never taught what to do with it.

So if we want our kids to benefit from the wealth we've built and we want *their* kids to benefit too, we need to be really intentional about it.

It's Not About Spoiling Them

For me personally, my kids will not be touching a dollar of my wealth until they can prove to me they're ready. Not just emotionally, but financially, mentally and practically.

I'm not doing this so they can skip the struggle and live on private jets eating Wagyu with gold flakes to look cool for their social media friends. I'm doing this so when the right moment comes and they've done the work to grow into strong, smart humans, my wealth can become a jetpack, not a set of handcuffs.

Here's the thing, the chase, the foundation, the struggle is the most interesting part of this book. Imagine this book without that rave and instead my parents just gave me the deposit? Imagine the crazy way I learned about life, money, wealth etc, if my parents just paid for a financial adviser and I didn't need to learn anything.

I'd probably be a degenerate, honestly.

My kids need to show me they understand money, how to manage it, how to multiply it, and how to make good decisions. I'll help guide them. I'll make sure they've got mentors around them. I'll teach them how to delay gratification and how to value people, not things. But if they don't prove to me by the day I die that they can manage it on my behalf, then I'm sorry, I'll be doing what's best for them, and that's donating it all to charity.

If they can prove it to me, then yeah, my wealth will launch them forward. If they can't, it's staying in the vault and going to charity.

The last thing I want is to hand over a multi-million dollar inheritance to someone who turns it into a gambling problem, a cocaine addiction or spends their days dressing like Jaden Smith at the 2025 Grammy Awards.

No way! That's not why I did what I did.

If you want your wealth to last, it's not about having a good Will or a family trust, it's about raising kids who understand money before they inherit it. That starts now. Teach them about saving, investing, delayed gratification, taking calculated risks, and surrounding themselves with people who've done what they want to do.

Let them see how you make decisions. Let them hear you talk about money in a healthy way. Let them be in the room when you're buying your next property, meeting your Accountant, or reviewing your investments.

That's how you build generational wealth that doesn't just last, it expands.

We're not just building portfolios for ourselves anymore.

We're building a foundation for our kids, and their kids, and the ones after that.

Giving Back:
Creating Impact with Property

Once you've taken care of yourself and your family, it's time to look outward. When most people first start investing in property, the goal is simple: security. Maybe freedom. Maybe early retirement. Maybe just proving to yourself and your family that you *can* do it.

But once you've got that foundation in place, and your own life is on solid ground, there comes a point where you start to think a little bigger. You start asking different questions.

What kind of impact can I have? How can I use this to help others? How can I give back without burning myself out or going broke?

That's where the real magic of property can show up, not just as a tool for wealth, but as a vehicle for impact.

What Giving Back Can Actually Look Like

It doesn't have to mean donating millions to charity or becoming a full-blown philanthropist. It could be as simple as:

- Providing high-quality, affordable rental housing in areas that actually need it
- Choosing to keep the rent reasonable rather than squeezing tenants for every last dollar
- Offering your time to mentor younger investors or people who never had financial role models
- Creating family trusts that help future generations access education, business opportunities or housing

» Supporting causes that align with your values, whether that's housing for DV survivors, veterans, indigenous families or youth homelessness

And yeah, if you *can* give large sums of money, go for it. But don't underestimate how powerful even the small acts are when they're done consistently.

I'm committed to more than just building wealth, I want to create meaningful change. A portion of all my clients fees goes directly to not-for-profit charities that provide shelter, support and a path forward for people experiencing homelessness. We also volunteer our time.

When my kids are older, they'll be involved even more so we can help them understand that wealth isn't about being greedy, it's about impact. You cannot impact your society when you're in survival mode.

Wealth in the hands of evil people can absolutely do a lot of evil.

But, Wealth in the hands of good people can do a lot of good for your community and society around you. That's the message that we aim to share with you and teach our kids.

Final Thoughts: *Your Next 12 Months*

Make the Next Year Count

You've just read through a lot of information; mindset, strategy, stories, wins, mistakes, hard truths and hopefully some laughs. But none of it matters unless you actually do something with it.

This is where it all comes together.

Right now, before life gets in the way, take a moment to do this:

Step 1: Write Down Your Goals

Not vague ideas. Actual, tangible goals.

- Do you want to buy your first property?
- Do you want to restructure your finances and finally get in control?
- Do you want to grow your portfolio?
- Do you want to secure your retirement plan?

Whatever it is, write it down.

Step 2: Break It Down Into Steps

Goals are useless unless they're broken into actions. If your goal is to buy a property, your steps might look like this:

- Speak to a Mortgage Broker and get clarity on borrowing power
- List all your current expenses and find areas to cut
- Set a savings target and divide it by 12 (that's your monthly goal)
- Research areas that align with your budget and future growth
- Speak with a Buyers Agent or someone who knows what they're doing
- Book in a planning session to map out your strategy
- Start executing

If it's not property, then the steps will look different, but there are always steps.

Step 3: Give Yourself 12 Months

That's it. Give yourself **one full year**.

12 months of insane focus. 12 months of saying no to distractions; Friday night drinks, weddings, birthdays (where you can), screen time. 12 months of making uncomfortable decisions, trying new things, and doing the extra work.

I've done this multiple times in my life, and I can tell you, 12 months is plenty of time to completely shift the trajectory of your life.

I bought my first property when I was still figuring out what I wanted from life. I completed my MBA in just over a year while working full time. I made the decision to move to Brisbane and met my wife within 12 months. I've travelled the world, built businesses, raised a family and created a life on my terms, all from focused 12-month sprints... but don't rush finding your partner, I just got lucky there :)

This stuff works if you work.

Step 4: Make the Call

Book the appointment. Have the conversation. Call the Mortgage Broker. Reach out to the Adviser. Speak with a Buyers Agent. Make the spreadsheet. Set the alarm earlier. Delete the crap off your phone that wastes your time.

The only person who can do this... is you.

Your next 12 months could be a blur of nothing... or they could be the most defining year of your life.

The choice is yours.

Now stop reading, and go build the future you know you're capable of.

I believe in you.

Genreless Books

Sharing stories by independent Australian writers, of all genres.

Genreless Books is an independent publishing house based in Australia, founded in 2025 by Australian writer–designer Liam Stritt. We support local writers with everything they need to turn their self-publishing dream into a reality.

Liam was delighted to bring *Property with Purpose* to life for Michael Shaw.

If you're a writer of any kind looking to self-publish, Liam offers total support throughout the journey, so you can share your story with confidence, and a kind human touch along the way.

Made in the USA
Monee, IL
12 November 2026

346b649a-9c4a-43e2-ad64-7538fc6acb70R01